"This is a book you'll treasure and go back to over and over again. It's convicting, funny, and wise. And even if you wince, it's profoundly biblical. Meet the real Jesus and you'll never be the same. And not only that, you'll rise up and call me blessed for having told you about it."

— STEVE BROWN, professor at Reformed Theological Seminary (Orlando), author, and teacher on the *Key Life* radio program

"There is an anxious question in the air: does church contribute anything positive to following Jesus? If you are asking this question, the late Michael Spencer is someone who felt your pain. If you have left the church to follow Jesus, and if you find him, Jesus will lead you to a community of fellow followers—call it what you will. *Mere Churchianity* will guide you along this path."

— BISHOP TODD HUNTER, Holy Trinity Anglican Church, author of *Giving Church Another Chance*

"Michael Spencer was a self-described 'post-evangelical' Christian. He pointed out what already was obvious to many: that too often, churches practice 'moralistic, culture-war religion.' And sadly, their members are 'church-shaped' rather than Jesus-shaped. Almost prophetic in his railing against the prosperity gospel and efforts to turn God into a 'convenient vending machine,' Spencer's book offers a timely and difficult reimagining of what living as a person of faith really means."

— JENNIFER GRANT, journalist, columnist for *The Chicago Tribune*

"*Mere Churchianity* expresses a brilliant empathy for those who are disillusioned with—and distant from—what evangelicalism has become. At the same time, Michael's writing is a clarion call to evangelicals to stop obscuring Jesus and his gospel. This book asks the most challenging question of all: does the body of Christ resemble Jesus?"

— JARED C. WILSON, pastor, author of *Your Jesus Is Too Safe*

"If you are satisfied with the way the church does Christianity in America, then you should back slowly away. However, if you are willing to be challenged, and maybe even infuriated, by Michael Spencer's analysis of evangelicalism, then read this book. You may or may not agree with him, but you will be forced to think and hopefully pray about how we engage those who have left our churches."

— DAVE BURCHETT, author of *When Bad Christians Happen to Good People*

"Every Christian, regardless if they're engaged in church or not, needs to read, discuss, and reread *Mere Churchianity*. Reading this book is like the best of Brennan Manning, Anne Lamott, and Philip Yancey all rolled into one literary experience. This is the best, most easily relatable book about following Jesus that I've read in at least ten years. What Michael left behind in words is nothing short of a gift."

— MATTHEW PAUL TURNER, author of *Churched* and *Hear No Evil*

"In this highly anticipated manifesto, Michael Spencer wrote for a generation that is struggling to figure out what it means to live out Jesus-shaped spirituality. Michael was familiar with the burdens of the dominating religious, political, and cultural norms that suffocate our everyday existence. *Mere Churchianity* delivers, and its message will live on through people who can't help but be changed by it."

— ANDREW MARIN, author of *Love Is an Orientation,* president of The Marin Foundation

"As someone who has been writing for years on the supremacy of Jesus Christ and its relationship to his church, I found the Christ-centeredness of this book to be profoundly refreshing. We have lost a choice servant of God in Michael, but heaven is the richer. I'm thankful that he left us this excellent contribution."

— FRANK VIOLA, author of *Jesus Manifesto, Reimagining Church,* and *Finding Organic Church*

"You will look far and wide before you find another Christian who speaks with as much honesty, insight, and foresight as Michael Spencer. I am very careful about the Christian books I recommend, but this one definitely makes the list. I am excited to have a book I can give my non-Christian friends that accurately portrays Jesus."

— JIM HENDERSON, author of *Evangelism Without Additives, Jim and Casper Go to Church,* and *The Outsider Interviews*

Finding Your Way Back to
Jesus-Shaped Spirituality

MERE CHURCHIANITY

MICHAEL
SPENCER
The Internet Monk

WATERBROOK
PRESS

MERE CHURCHIANITY
PUBLISHED BY WATERBROOK PRESS
12265 Oracle Boulevard, Suite 200
Colorado Springs, Colorado 80921

All Scripture quotations, unless otherwise indicated, are taken from The Holy Bible, English
Standard Version, copyright © 2001 by Crossway Bibles, a division of Good News Publishers.
Used by permission. All rights reserved. Scripture quotations marked (NLT) are taken from the
Holy Bible, New Living Translation, copyright © 1996, 2004. Used by permission of Tyndale
House Publishers Inc., Wheaton, Illinois 60189. All rights reserved.

Names and details in some anecdotes and stories have been changed to protect the identities of
the persons involved.

ISBN 978-0-307-45917-6
ISBN 978-0-307-45918-3 (electronic)

Published in the United States by WaterBrook Multnomah, an imprint of the Crown Publishing
Group, a division of Random House Inc., New York.

WATERBROOK and its deer colophon are registered trademarks of Random House Inc.

Library of Congress Cataloging-in-Publication Data
Spencer, Michael, 1956–
    Mere churchianity : finding your way back to Jesus-shaped spirituality / Michael Spencer
(The Internet Monk). — 1st ed.
        p. cm.
Includes bibliographical references (p.   ).
    ISBN 978-0-307-45917-6 — ISBN 978-0-307-45918-3 (electronic) 1. Spirituality. 2. Jesus
Christ. 3. Christian life. I. Title.
    BV4501.3.S6613 2010
    248.0973 — dc22

                                2010010531

Printed in the United States of America
2010 — First Edition

10 9 8 7 6 5 4 3 2 1

SPECIAL SALES
Most WaterBrook Multnomah books are available at special quantity discounts when
purchased in bulk by corporations, organizations, and special-interest groups. Custom
imprinting or excerpting can also be done to fit special needs. For information, please e-mail
SpecialMarkets@WaterBrookMultnomah.com or call 1-800-603-7051.

Contents

Acknowledgments

Everything in this book has been written with a specific group of people in mind: friends and fellow Christians who have abandoned the church for various reasons. I cannot name them, nor would it be appropriate, but their journeys have animated my mind, heart, and keyboard on every page. I love them, and they remain my fellow pilgrims. I hope I have honored their integrity and continuing journey with Jesus.

In November 2000, I started a blog called the Internet Monk. Today a community of many thousands has made my writing part of their journey. Without these readers and encouragers from every Christian tradition, I would not be an author. To them, I owe this book.

My wife, Denise, is the answer to the question, I want to know what love is.

My children, Noel Cordle and Clay Spencer, never fail to make me glad that I am a father. I hope this book will honor their devotion to Christ and remind them of a dad's heart when I am gone.

My parents were humble, simple people who loved me. My father walked away from the church when I was small because of a divorce when he was a young man. He loved God from outside the church. He only heard me preach five times.

My mom loved the church, but her devotion to missional, servant living outside the church—working in a clothing ministry, assisting the homebound, always sharing her car and money with those needing help—has been an increasing revelation to me of where God's true servants are often to be found.

My in-laws, Cordell and Billie Day, have always been treasures for Denise and me as we have lived a life in ministry. Their constant support is a great gift.

This book was born when Jeff Dunn called me and said he'd read "Our Problem with Grace," a piece I posted on my blog. Jeff said I should write a book. No one has a better agent, and no one has a better friend in his agent. Thank you, Jeff, for making a dream come true.

My editor, Ron Lee, is a pro with a gentle touch and a firm sense of direction. I wouldn't want to edit my own writing, but Ron has made the experience a pleasure. Thank you, Ron, for all your hard work.

Thanks to the Boar's Head Tavern fellows, who have been a virtual Christian family for going on eight years now. They are peerless examples of rejoicing in the good that happens to others.

Special thanks to constant encouragers: David Head, Bill Haynes, Jared Wilson, Steve Brown, Andrew Marin, Michael Patton, Mike Hertenstein, Mark and Judy Palmieri, Eric Landry, Keith Todd, Bob Browning, Peter Matthews, Alan Creech, Paul Davidson, Mack Stiles, Tom Meacham, Bill Whittaker, John Lovett, Darrell Mitchell, Jim Chinn, and especially Dan Stockton.

Thanks to the thousands of students and fellow school staff who have listened to my preaching and teaching for the last eighteen years.

Some of my best friends have gone on but showed the way before they left: Barkley Moore, J. V. Case, Henry Walters, Michael McGarvey, Tom Rogers, Ed Beavin, Henry Schafer, and especially W. O. Spencer.

Thanks to Paul Duke and Gerard Howell for showing me what ministry with humanity and integrity was all about.

Publisher's Note

In the fall of 2009, Michael Spencer and I were working out the best structure for this book. He would send me a few chapters at a time, and I would read them as soon as they showed up in my Outlook inbox. I loved the directness of his writing, his humor and passion, and the boldness of his message.

We had made good progress on editing and sequencing the chapters when Michael said of his book, "I could lose my job over this." He was only half joking. I could well imagine that some who supported the Christian school where Michael was campus minister might not appreciate his unvarnished views on the church. But he was not a writer—nor a shepherd—who would dilute his message to pacify potential critics.

Michael had written the entire book and completed his revisions before medical tests showed that he had cancer. The disease, and not opposition to his message, is the tragedy that interrupted his work at Oneida Baptist Institute. Cancer put a stop to his seventeen years of teaching and disrupted his years of pioneering pastoral ministry in the lives of hundreds of thousands who followed his blog (www.internetmonk.com).

I learned today that Michael, in his last months on earth, kept a journal. At the end of this book you can read one of the entries. It is characteristic of Michael's devotion to God—an unflinching affirmation and a benediction. But before you get to the epilogue, allow your thinking to be challenged and your life changed by Michael's passionate message that Jesus is now and always the Alpha and Omega—not just in theory or doctrine, but in your life. Every day. "I am the Alpha and the Omega, the beginning and the end. To the thirsty I will give from the spring of the water of life without payment" (Revelation 21:6).

Mere Churchianity is the only book Michael wrote. These eighteen chapters contain the last words he approved for publication. If you don't already know the voice of the Internet Monk, you will discover that his words are wise, humorous, compassionate, challenging, and welcoming. It was my privilege to be Michael's editor. Now it is your privilege to read and discuss his words and to be blessed.

Ron R. Lee

Senior Editor, WaterBrook Press

April 2010

The Dairy Queen Incident

This book began with an atheist in a Dairy Queen, thirty-three years ago.

I was a twenty-year-old college student and youth minister at a Baptist church in Kentucky. Most Sunday nights I took my rowdy and unspiritual youth group out for fast food as a reward for their endurance of church and Sunday school that day. A new Dairy Queen had just opened in our community, and I took the kids there for burgers or, if any of them preferred, soft ice cream.

We all loved DQ, so we stayed awhile. We bought our food, ate our food, and acted like a typical rowdy and unspiritual church youth group. The biggest stress of the evening for me, as the responsible adult, was some kid dumping an entire shaker of salt on a table. Having attended public schools and spent my share of time in school cafeterias, I thought nothing of it. I just left the mess for the help to clean up. We had paid for our food and, as far as I knew, departed the DQ without serious incident.

On Wednesday morning I received a letter from a girl who was working at the Dairy Queen the previous Sunday evening. I don't have that letter today, but I have never forgotten its basic message. Allow me to paraphrase:

> Mr. Spencer,
>
> You don't know me, but I am Jane Doe, and I work at the
> Dairy Queen on Hartford Road. I was working the front this past

Sunday night when your youth group invaded and abused our restaurant for an hour. You probably have no idea how rude they were and how much time and trouble their behavior and destruction of property caused our business because, like every other youth minister I see in our store, you are clueless about anyone who isn't in your group and blind to the behavior of your students.

You also probably don't know that I am a member of your church, but for the past year I have been an atheist. The reason is very simple: Christians like you have convinced me that God is a myth, an excuse used by religious people to mistreat others. As long as there are people like you and your youth group, I'll never come to church or believe in God again. You are petty, selfish, and arrogant. I would rather be an atheist, no matter what the consequences, than have people like you accept me just because I was a "Christian."

I know you won't contact me, and you'll probably throw this letter away and forget it, but just remember that when you and your youth group are being destructive and inconsiderate, there are people like me looking at you and making up our minds whether God even exists. If you are all I have to go on, he doesn't and never will.

Sincerely,

Jane Doe

Reading this letter, many of you are probably reacting much as I did: here's some miserable, rejected girl with a chip on her shoulder, mad at her parents for making her go to church. She's probably mad about other things in her life too and needs someone to blame. So she takes it out on the youth group and on God. C'mon, it was just a little spilled salt. Really, how self-righteous does a person have to be to blame the representatives of God for her own rejection and pain?

If you were thinking something like that, you may be right. Or you could be dead wrong.

To show you where my head was at, I didn't go back to apologize. I wrote her off as a sad, isolated atheist with issues. I probably told some of the youth group members about her letter and had a big laugh at her hypersensitivity. At the time, I was fully capable of taking a letter like that and waving it around during a sermon, using it as an example of how miserable atheists are. I'm sure it crossed my mind that the presence of Christians in her workplace may have brought her "under conviction by the Holy Spirit" for her unbelief. Surely she had no legitimate reason to criticize my youth group.

Back then, I was a paid expert in churchianity. I knew how to impress the home crowd. I used all the right words, and I knew what buttons to push to rally the troops. Sadly, I knew very little about Jesus and the life he calls his followers to live.

Lots of Christians are like I was. They would find it easy to blame an atheist for not acting like a Christian, while failing to act like a Christian in the presence of an atheist. I did such things too many times to recall. I used the girl's honest, heartfelt critique as an easy pitch to hit in front of a clubby, misguided Christian audience. I bought into all the accepted assumptions: Christians are right, the other guys are wrong, and since we're in the right, we have nothing to worry about.

———

I held on to that safe place of smug comfort for many years, and then I realized it wasn't all that comfortable any longer. It has been more than thirty years since I read Jane Doe's letter, and I still can't get it out of my mind. Today I see her insights in a very different light. As a cocky, twenty-something preacher boy, I could easily write off a woman who didn't believe the truth. But now, in my fifties and bearing the scars of life, struggle, sin, and loss, I respect that young atheist more than I do a long list of high-profile Christian leaders.

Jane Doe is emblematic of something I now believe very deeply: unbelievers see some things about life, integrity, and consistency *much more clearly* than Christians do.

On that Sunday evening in Dairy Queen, my youth group probably was out of control. They were likely rude to the help, possibly foulmouthed and insulting. They vandalized a saltshaker and made a mess for another person to clean up. I gave them a pass. I even thought it was funny. The prevailing tone of that evening was a selfish, unthinking party with all of us—adults and kids alike—caring a lot more about what we wanted than what another person might be thinking. And we didn't care who would have to clean up after us. Our understanding and practice of churchianity endorsed such behavior.

We had fun that night, but did we invite Jesus Christ to the party? I don't remember him being there. In fact, I don't think he mattered to us at all that evening. We were taking a break from the religious stuff.

The people working behind the counter? The guy who cleared the tables? The other customers? They might as well have not existed.

An atheist girl, having left the church behind and now looking back with eyes and ears sensitized to the Christian game, saw through our act with sobering clarity. She tried to do me a favor by telling me I had lost touch with Jesus. An atheist girl cared enough to tell me that my credibility as a Christian was zero, because there was nothing of Jesus about me and my students. All we had was distasteful pretense.

It took an atheist to tell me, perhaps for the first time, that I was not a Jesus-shaped person, no matter what I claimed to believe as a Christian. But I was so sure of what I believed, so convinced of the rightness of my religion, that I chose to ignore the truth she spoke.

———

When you read the title of this book, you might have thought it's a book for Christians, and that's fine, because I am a Christian. I have no doubt that Christians want to hear what I have to say. However, this is not a Christian book in the time-honored tradition. I'm not going to tell Christians to be nicer, care more, help other people, be generous, try to forgive, do more for God, and so on, so that we can be better witnesses for Jesus.

I have good reasons for staying off the standard Christian-book path. It was churchianity—the "do more, be better, look good for God's sake" variety—that turned me and my youth group into a room full of jerks. So if you're a Christian, by all means read this book. You will find an approach to following Jesus that doesn't ask you to do more while pretending to be righteous. I think you'll like it.

But I'm not writing to church members who are happy where they're at or to Christians who are heavily invested in the success and propagation of the church as an organization. I'm writing instead to those who may still be associated with the church but no longer buy into much of what the church says. Not because they doubt the reality of God, but because they doubt that the church is really representing Jesus.

I'm writing to people on the inside who are about to leave or have already left. I'm writing to those who are standing in the foyer of the church, ready to walk out, yet taking one last look around. They haven't seen the reality of Jesus in a long time, but they can't stop believing he is here. Somewhere. And they're unsure what it will mean to strike out on their own.

Mere Churchianity is written for people who have come to the end of the road with the church but who can't entirely walk away from Jesus. In the wreckage of a church-shaped religious faith, the reality of Jesus of Nazareth persists and calls out to them. I'm talking to those who have left, those who will leave, those who might as well leave, and those who don't know why they are still hanging around.

And I'm writing to the outsiders who might be drawn to God if it weren't for Christians.

—

Jesus-shaped spirituality has nothing to do with churchianity. Following Jesus does not require you to pledge allegiance to a religious institution. In fact, the track record of Christianity as an organization leads us to ask: What would it be like if Christianity were about Christ? What if all the pieces were in place and Jesus was the result? What if Christians were becoming more—not less—like Jesus? What would atheists see if Christianity were something Jesus himself would recognize?

That letter from the girl who worked at Dairy Queen contained an invisible paragraph. It would have been easy to see it, if I had bothered to look. The invisible paragraph says this:

> You see, Mr. Spencer, even though I've left the church and the faith you are pushing, I still know a bit about Jesus. Christianity ought to be about Jesus, and with you, it's not. It's something else entirely. If Christians were at all about Jesus, if they were enough like him that even a visit to the Dairy Queen would be a place to serve Jesus and love people, then I might have some hope again that the church isn't full of liars. But Christians like you make me never want to hear about Christianity again.

When I was growing up in church, we were constantly being told how important it was that people "see Jesus in us." We sang those words, and the preacher preached sermons using that theme. Being a "good witness" for Jesus was the constant bottom line.

Looking back at what formed me spiritually, I'm confronted with an incredible irony. While we talked about presenting Jesus to the world around us, unfortunately the following was true:

- We had almost no idea what Jesus was like. We did not study him. We did not ask questions. We were arrogant and certain.

- We assumed that being in church would make us like Jesus. Church programs and events filled our days, and everyone assumed that more church equaled more Jesus.
- We seldom studied anything in the Bible with the purpose of seeing how it connected to Jesus. The Bible was approached and taught as a collection of atomized verses, and no one ever linked its many parts to its one great theme: Jesus and his gospel.
- We often were ungracious and unloving to people who didn't believe what we did. Incredibly, we sometimes dished out mistreatment in the name of Jesus.
- We knew very little about what Jesus was doing on earth besides dying and rising again two thousand years ago. We were certain that being his followers meant that we didn't do the things sinners did. When anyone suggested we might be self-righteous, morally corrupt Pharisees, we were offended. After all, what did the critics know? They weren't Christians.
- We assumed that Jesus bought into our idea of what was important in life. All anyone had to do was read the Bible to see that we were in the right and everyone else was wrong.

From that, you can see why it was easy to go to a Dairy Queen on a Sunday night, act like an ungrateful gang of spoiled suburban brats, ignore the people who served us, leave a mess behind, and still feel we were authentic representatives of Jesus because we were "good church people."

Here is the truth: Far from being Jesus-shaped Christians, we were church shaped. In fact, we were deniers of Jesus. We were frighteningly close to being Judas.

The girl working behind the counter pointed all this out to me more than three decades ago, but I wasn't listening. Today I'm paying attention, and this book is my repentance. It's a good time to get started.

PART 1

THE JESUS DISCONNECT

People Leaving the Church and the Church Leaving Jesus

When Church Signs Lie

I have lived in Kentucky for almost fifty years. If you travel our highways, you'll see a variety of lovely scenery. You will also see a variety of road signs, one of which says Deer Crossing. The attention-grabbing yellow sign features a black silhouette drawing of a deer crossing the road.

I've seen all kinds of deer along Kentucky's roads: I've seen bucks and does; I've seen small herds; I've seen deer standing in the road; I've noticed them a safe distance from the road, drinking from a creek; I've seen them running through fields; and I've seen them dead after a collision with a car.

I have never, as far as I know, seen a deer cross a road at or near a Deer Crossing sign.

I admit that I've never packed a lunch and sat down by a Deer Crossing sign to conduct a formal study, but I've discussed this with a good number of rural Kentuckians. They agree with my conclusion that deer don't seem to cross roads at Deer Crossing signs.

Do deer read the signs and then decide to take an alternate route? Do they avoid posted areas out of deer contrariness? Or, more likely, are the signs installed by people who have never paid attention to deer and their habits?

Deer Crossing signs seem to mean there are deer and they do cross roads. Somewhere. Sometime.

We have another kind of sign where I live. You have probably seen them where you live as well. They are church signs that promise, in effect, that Jesus is there. Elvis might have left the building, ladies and gentlemen, but not Jesus. Or so the sign makers would have you believe.

Sometimes it's a catchy slogan, other times it's a straightforward announcement: "We have Jesus in here." But is Jesus really there behind the church sign? He might be, or maybe he's not.

I believe Jesus is alive, just as Christians announce to the world every Easter. He was raised by the power of God and is alive and reigning over the universe. He said, "I am with you always,"[1] and I believe he's alive to do exactly what he promised.

I've seen what he can do. I've seen the evidence of changed lives, amazing love, and the Kingdom of God rescuing this broken world. At the same time, Jesus seems to be a bit like an east Kentucky whitetail. He doesn't show up just because someone plants a sign in front of a building saying he'll be there at eleven o'clock Sunday morning. He's more elusive and much less predictable than the people who put up these signs suspect.

I'm not cynical about the church. You won't find me trashing the red-brick house of worship downtown, the one that claims to be first at something—Methodist, Presbyterian, Lutheran, Baptist, Assembly of God, or Congregational. You won't hear me say that the only people who really get it are the ones who are the drawn-to-my-hip gathering of enlightened Jesus-followers. I think Jesus shows up in a lot of places where we might not expect to see him, even church.

A few times I've met him at one of the buildings with a sign out front. I've also discovered that when he told one church in the book of Revelation that he was standing outside, looking for even one person who cared enough to bother opening the door to connect with him, he was telling the truth.[2]

Jesus is always there for his people. People don't have to hunt him down or beg to get his attention. Jesus loves the world he created and everyone in it. According to the Bible, he loves the people who have trusted and followed him like a husband loves his bride.[3]

But if you were to pack a lunch and sit in a lawn chair right next to one of those Jesus Is in the Building church signs, you may have much the same experience I've had with Kentucky Deer Crossing signs. Nice sign, but no deer. Nice church, but where's Jesus?

DOES THE SIGN ALWAYS LIE?

It's easier to be negative than to say something constructive. (Just ask a few teenagers what they think of their parents.) So I could tell you that the folks who bring you the Jesus Is Here signs are misguided, misled, and mostly mistaken. Or I could tell you that, in many cases, they are people who would sacrifice themselves to save your life. I have known church people in every season of my life. They have picked me up more than once, when no one else would bother with me. The same people who place black letters on the Jesus Is Here signs have been living signs of the reality of Jesus for me.

Sometimes Jesus is definitely there, evidenced in the lives of church-going people. So it's never easy for me to say out loud that, for millions of us, the Jesus Is Here sign can't be trusted. And to add that we have excellent reasons to be suspicious when we read the sign.

I didn't come to this conclusion easily. I want to believe Christians when they say Jesus makes an appearance on their stage every weekend. For me it has been a hard journey to say "probably not." I'm skeptical. It's like those e-mails I get from an African royal who needs my assistance in transferring millions of dollars to an American bank. Hard experience and the testimony of others tell me not to bite. Likewise, a lifetime of being in church has caused me, sadly, to check behind the sign to see what's really there.

When I hear churchianity-oriented Christians say, "Jesus wants us to build a multimillion-dollar facility to grow into," I'm skeptical.

When I hear a church announce, "Miracle and healing revival! The sick cured every night. Bring your loved ones," I have to wonder how they can schedule a miracle.

When I hear the church at large say, "We have the vision and mission of Jesus at heart," I ask why it's not more evident.

Whenever I hear a congregation insist that it exists to help the hurting, I find myself doubting.

When I hear preachers talk about waging the culture war, getting involved in politics, and needing to save America, I'm skeptical about their claim to be speaking for Jesus.

I hate to say these things, because over the past half-century a lot of church people have been a lifeline to me. But for some time now, the Jesus Is Here sign doesn't work any longer.

LOOKING BEHIND THE SIGN

Behind the Jesus Is Here sign is an expanding moralistic, culture-war religion that doesn't look or sound at all like Jesus' new-covenant Kingdom. Does Jesus really care whether a teacher is allowed to lead kids in prayer in a public-school classroom or if an Alabama courtroom is decorated with the Ten Commandments?

And then there are the religious record keepers and statisticians. Behind the Jesus Is Here sign are seemingly endless versions of the church-growth obsession that has gripped evangelicalism for more than half a century. No longer do most Christians question the assumption that bigger is always better; God has made it clear he prefers a gigantic church with enormous facilities. Sports arenas are converted into worship centers, and thousands of pastors can't stop imitating Rick Warren, right down to the shirt. What would Jesus do if he were confronted with an escalator inside a shopping-mall-sized megachurch? Would he let it take him for a ride?

Behind the Jesus Is Here sign are too many narcissistic competitors in what has rightly been called "the worship wars," a consumerist competition to draw a bigger audience into a fog of Jesus-lite entertainment. How long could Jesus remain on his feet when directed to sing fifteen consecutive worship choruses, each one only seven words long and repeated twenty-three times?

Behind the Jesus Is Here sign are too many pastors with ambitions Jesus wouldn't recognize: ambitions to fly their own jets and put their smiling faces on book covers, morning-commute coffee mugs, and every television screen on the planet. Would Jesus invest in eighty acres of prime suburban real estate so he could build a "campus" as a way to change the world?

Behind the Jesus Is Here sign is a health, wealth, and prosperity "gospel" that removes God from the status of sovereign Lord and turns him into a convenient vending machine. Insert a prayer in the slot, pull the lever, and get a great life now. This type of thinking is big among Christians, but it shows very little respect for the omnipotent God who created the universe. Christians who worship the celestial vending machine assume that God is all about giving them more stuff and making them feel better. I wonder if Jesus mentioned promises of earthly goodies to the repentant criminal hanging on the cross next to him.

Behind the Jesus Is Here sign is unchecked consumerist idolatry and enslavement to our culture's economic expectations. Check the parking lot. You'd think the church had invested heavily in German engineering, luxury SUVs, and petroleum futures.

Behind the Jesus Is Here sign is often a near-vacuum of discipleship. Jesus-shaped discipleship produces people whose lives, habits, commitments, and words resemble Jesus more than the cultural ideals of comfort, convenience, and economic prosperity. Would Jesus really win the Most Likely to Succeed award at his school?

Behind the Jesus Is Here sign, Jesus is used as a symbol to approve what we already are, to bless what we are already pursuing, and to prefer the people we are most similar to. Given his reported endorsement of white, suburban, Reagan-era conservatism, I have to wonder if Jesus was a fan of *Family Ties*.

Behind the Jesus Is Here sign...you really don't know if Jesus is there or not. What if Jesus has left the building? What if Jesus is standing outside, looking at the Jesus Is Here sign in much the same way you do? With skepticism.

GOD ISN'T ON MY GOOGLE MAP

If you grew up in church, like I did, you were told all the time that God doesn't live in buildings. They always said it with straight faces, but outside the ICU, the funeral home, and the dinner-hour blessing, they never acted like they believed a word of it.

In the religious culture I grew up in, God was always in the sanctuary of First Denominational Church, situated on a downtown street corner across from a bank or another church. He was there when we were there, and he was doing whatever we said he was doing. Like a genie in a bottle, God showed up when we invoked him. It was easy to catalog his actions inside the church building; it got a lot harder when we tried to think about God doing things outside of regular worship services. Let's see, he's running the universe, answering prayers, and...

The standard practice of preachers linking God's work so closely to church programs and priorities had a devastating effect on Christians who gave up on the church. For them, leaving the church meant leaving Jesus behind in the church. God was so closely linked to the building that it seemed he was the property of the congregation. The church acted as if it had God on salary, with him keeping regular office hours and even being on call whenever he might be needed.

That claim on God and his activities, ironically, helps explain the empty pews in most of our churches.

For a long time people believed the church sign that said God was there. Or maybe it was that they desperately wanted to believe the sign, so they showed up on Sunday mornings looking for God. They would leave the building an hour later having found a robed choir, a slick speaker at the podium, a plea for money, and some beautiful stained glass. But no God. Feeling cheated and lied to, and maybe a little embarrassed about being so gullible, they felt they had to leave. But they still wanted God.

Eventually, leaving the god who sponsored the religious agenda was, for many people, the only way to hold on to an authentic idea of God. Leaving the Jesus who was said to be in the building was the only way to believe in a Jesus who wasn't confined to a building.

Research on America's religious landscape and the widespread changes in religious affiliation tells a fascinating story. Twenty-eight percent of adult Americans have left the faith of their childhood, some in favor of a different religion and others choosing no religion at all. One in four Americans aged eighteen to twenty-nine are not affiliated with a religion. And among all adult Americans who report no religious affiliation (16.1 percent), more than half are people who grew up in a religious home. (Among the religiously unaffiliated, 4 percent describe themselves as atheist or agnostic.) Interestingly, the group that has shown the most growth through changes in religious affiliation is "the unaffiliated."[4]

With the number of people who are changing their religious affiliation on the increase, how do we explain the growing numbers of nonreligious people who aren't atheist or agnostic? At the very least, they must still have a good measure of curiosity about God, so why did they turn away from religion?

I think I know why. They are the millions of people who could no longer believe in the God of American churchianity—whether Catholic, Orthodox, mainline Protestant, Pentecostal, charismatic, or evangelical. The God behind the labels and the church signs didn't look like God to them, so they went looking elsewhere.

But they still believe…something; they haven't completely let go.

THE GOD SEEKERS

Who are the God seekers?

They are divorced, married, and single. They are educated, self-taught, heterosexual, and gay. They are professionals, blue-collar, and seeking honest meaning in life. They are young, idealistic, and critical of tradition. They are unmoved by the culture war, they are socially progressive, and they are burned out. They are turned off by manipulative evangelism and the stubborn inability of religious people to see that life is not always black and white. Some are angry, apathetic, and cynical about religion. Many have moved on, moved off, and moved away.

They've turned their backs on the God behind the sign, the genie in the bottle, the Jesus under contract to the church. They have left all that behind. But they are still carrying around…something. And it's something important. Many of them call it *spirituality*. (More on that word later, but don't forget their strong connection to spirituality.)

Jesus talked about this sort of spirituality in one of his most interesting stories. It's often referred to as the prodigal son. Jesus never called it that—he didn't name his stories—and the word *prodigal* doesn't register with most people today. Some have called it the story of the two sons or the two brothers. Others have called it the story of the waiting father.

I think it's God's story and our story, disguised as the tale of a dysfunctional family. God makes use of a lot of dysfunctional families in the Bible to talk about who we are and to describe the truth about the human situation.

While you can read the story in the gospel according to Luke, chapter 15, I'd like to retell it in my own words.

In the first part of the story, a father has two adult sons who live with him. That's how we started out. God was our Father, and we were in a family relationship with him.

Then, in chapter 2, the younger son tells Dad to hand over his financial inheritance now, while the son is young and stupid, so he can go do a little living. Dad, inexplicably, hands the money over, and the son hits the road for Vegas, Amsterdam, and Mardi Gras. This kind of stunt is fairly common with parents today, but in Jesus' time people would have wondered why Dad didn't send the boy to live with the goats.

The reason the father acts so strangely is that chapter 2 of this tale is our human story. We've told God to hand over the world—and our lives—to us, so we can demonstrate that we're big kids who don't need God to take care of us. God doesn't stop us from being wayward, selfish children. He lets us go. As Dr. Phil says, "How's that working out for you?"

In chapter 3 the younger son spends the cash, gets kicked out of the party, and winds up in a pigpen looking at muddy corncobs as a tasty alternative to starvation. In case you didn't notice, this bears more than a passing resemblance to what the Bible and experience tells us life looks and feels like when we're estranged from God. Note that for a period of time, the younger brother would have told you he was having a great time. Sound familiar?

In chapter 4 our boy decides that his dad could help him escape his pigpen lifestyle, but he doesn't want to deal with the full implications of his stupidity. So he creates a plan for apologizing to his father, whom he (rightly) assumes will be angry. That plan includes negotiating the son's new role in the family—that of servant. He will live out back and be useful, but he won't be a son any longer.

His plan should sound familiar to all of us, since it is the religious answer to our problem as human beings. It seems like the perfect solution, since it's our idea. But it's never God's idea, since he's not into religion.

Religion is our negotiation with God to try to get his help in exchange for our good behavior. We promise to do what we're told, and we expect God to reward us. This is a straightforward business arrangement, and we fully expect it to work. Meanwhile, we talk about being God's child as if we're family. But in our performance-for-reward arrangement, things don't operate on grace. Under the rules of religion, God is kept at arm's length and expected to be involved only to the degree that he gives us what we think we deserve.

The contrast between relationship and religion is obvious: beloved son or begrudging slave? We all would prefer the former, and we resent that the church has given us religion that leads to the latter. But even if you have left the church, it's unlikely that you left this chapter of the story. Humans are religious by nature, and our natural attraction to religion causes us to manufacture a god that operates according to our sense of right and wrong. Our god is glad to negotiate with us and on our terms.

Now back to our story. In chapter 5 the younger son returns home. Before he gets to the house, his father runs down the road to confront him. But instead of applying a baseball bat to the punk, the father embraces his son, weeps over him, and won't even allow the son to make his pitch for a life of servitude in exchange for three squares a day. Instead, Dad says, "This boy will be treated as a returning hero!" The father orders up the biggest party the neighborhood has ever seen.

JESUS, NOT CHURCHIANITY

Chapter 5, in which God refuses to negotiate with the wayward son, is the gospel, the Good News, the Best News, in fact. God will not play by our rules or be boxed in by our religion. He gets angry over our disobedience, but then he finds a way to get around his own rules and forgives screwups like the ungrateful son. The Father loves doing things like that.

The final chapter of this story features the strait-laced, do-the-right-thing older son, who is outraged and pouting. He has done everything right, as far as it's possible, and all the thanks he gets is an invitation to his younger brother's party. He can't believe his father actually forgave the brat. Can't anybody see how much better a son he is than the younger brother, who made a mess of his life and the family's reputation?

The father, as one would expect, tells the older son that he should be more like his father. In other words, the older brother needs to forgive the younger brother and go enjoy the party.

The older brother is caught up in churchianity, following the rules and conforming to expectations. But churchianity never wins in an argument with God. In Jesus' story, God forgives a major-league failure and throws him a party. Religion wants justice, but the Father knows that what is needed is grace and mercy.

Which leads me to ask, When millions of people walk away from the church that has a sign out front saying Jesus is inside, what are they walking away from?

Are they the younger son, walking away from God because they want to indulge their sin without the Father seeing what they're doing? Have they decided they want to run their own lives without interference from God? Or are they walking away from the churchianity of the older brother, with its insistence on conformity, outward appearance, and duty?

Are the people who run away, walk away, drift away, or lose their way really abandoning Jesus and the Good News? Or are they walking away from a church that has become disconnected from Jesus and all he stands for? Are they walking away from the empty promises spelled out on a church sign?

Perhaps the leavers and quitters are sending a message about Jesus that Christians need to take to heart. Perhaps churchianity has done more to alienate people from Christianity than all the best-selling books written by angry atheists. It is clear that the church has overadvertised something it has lost, and it's time to answer some questions about the Jesus who doesn't live behind the church signs.

The Jesus Disconnect

I'm a fan of Major League Baseball and the Cincinnati Reds. The Reds have a great tradition but haven't won the World Series since 1990. My interest in the team does not achieve the level of insanely loyal fan devotion associated with teams such as the Brewers or the Cubs. But still, it's a calling that requires a high tolerance for pain, despair, and tragedy.

One of the benefits of being a Reds fan is the easy acceptance of the fact that my team has major and ongoing problems (i.e., they pretty much suck most of the time). I am acclimated to breathtaking errors. I'm accustomed to watching my team blow a lead and give away a game in the bottom of the ninth. Management decisions that boggle the brain and suffocate all logic are frequent points of discussion and sources of angst for the Reds fan.

If my team wins half its games, I believe the Millennium has begun. Should the Reds make the play-offs, I would expect aliens to land at second base and introduce themselves to both teams during the seventh-inning stretch. If the Reds were to win the World Series, I would assume that hell was on ice-skating holiday and pigs were circling every airport in the world. It's not hard for me, or for thousands of other Reds fans, to admit that our beloved baseball franchise has fallen into a sad state.

If you're ever around evangelical Christians, though, you realize they have the opposite problem. They believe their ship is listing to one side because it gives them a more interesting look at the iceberg. Evangelicals believe that people who distance themselves from the church are not disenchanted but are "under conviction of the Holy Spirit." Christians are convinced that the generally low opinion people have of them—such as not wanting Christians as neighbors and trying to avoid having a conversation with Christians—is because people can't deal with the uncomfortable truth about Jesus. Evangelicals believe the growing numbers of young adults who grew up in church-attending families and then abandoned the ship of faith is the fault of Hollywood, liberals, rock music, and sex.

Riiight.

THE COMING EVANGELICAL COLLAPSE

In 2009 I wrote an essay published in the *Christian Science Monitor.* It was titled, innocently enough, "The Coming Evangelical Collapse."[1] For almost two months after it appeared in print, I waded through a massive media reaction to my prediction that within two decades, American evangelicalism would become a house emptied of half its occupants.

The responses covered the spectrum, from an open embrace to unbounded rage. Political liberals, secularists, atheists, and various nut jobs loved it. Christians who were, like me, feeling homeless in the confused and confusing world of evangelicalism resonated with my analysis and forecast. Many who had watched their churches descend into irrelevance found what I was predicting easy to affirm.

But then, of course, there were the convinced evangelicals, Christians who have too much to lose by admitting their movement has lost its bearings. They wrote letters and called on the phone, asking in amazement: "What are you talking about? Collapse? Decline? Everything is great in my church! We have six services! You should meet my cool pastor. We've got bigger crowds than ever. We're winning!"

This self-induced feelgoodism didn't surprise me. If you've left or pondered leaving the church, you probably aren't surprised by it either.

Christians in America seem to be living in a movie where they have written every scene to make themselves look like heroes. They've rigged the plot so their critics are always wrong and they will always win in the end.

If they are winners, what do the winners look like? Check out the massive facilities, celebrity pastors, and Christian media! Look at the stadium events, political clout, and private schools—K through 12! How about movies such as *The Passion of the Christ* and *Fireproof*? Look at the large numbers of people who agree with the militant Christian opposition to abortion and gay rights, including abominable civil unions!

"Coming 'collapse' of American evangelicalism?" "What was Michael Spencer talking about?" "He's a hardened cynic and wouldn't know a church-growth strategy if it was floating in his coffee." "The best thing for all of us is to avoid him and similar naysayers."

These responses reveal the attitudes of churchianity. There is no question that institutional Christianity still appeals to many optimistic Christians. They've created a movement by using a grade card that gives them consistent straight As. The grading system gives high marks to a few strong points and completely ignores what is painfully obvious in organized Christianity—the selective blindness, the unwarranted self-confidence, the smugness of shallow certainty.

It's a scorecard that overlooks completely the most basic thing that should be true about Christians—a meaningful connection to Jesus. The evangelical scorecard, however, fails to recognize the damning evidence that the rest of us can't overlook: a disconnection from Jesus; something I call "the Jesus Disconnect."

THEY VOTED WITH THEIR FEET

What evangelicals in North America call Christianity is, ironically, largely disconnected from Jesus as he appears in the four Gospels. I have argued for the past decade that American Christianity has evolved into a movement that Jesus would not recognize if he were to show up next Sunday.

And it's not just the rituals and assumptions and values that are off-base. The spirituality itself that comes out of contemporary Christianity is largely unrelated to Jesus. You don't have to believe me; all you need do is look at the statistics on who attends church, who used to attend, and who swears they will never attend again. Thousands, and possibly millions, of people are walking away from any association with the religion known as traditional Christianity.

Evangelical Christians have numbed their souls with toxic amounts of denial regarding their movement's loss of connection to Jesus. Not because the evidence is not there, and not because their own spiritual emptiness isn't shouting at many of them. Instead, it's because their interpretative grid shunts them off onto side roads and often into the ditch. It diverts them from the obvious truth regarding the church's spiritual bankruptcy. Why have so many young adults turned their backs on the church? There has to be a reason other than premarital sex, cheap beer, and great Sunday-morning programming on television.

People who have attended church since they were born and been active in all sorts of Christian ministries are abandoning ship. And sadly, many of those who have remained on board are convinced that the people who fled for their spiritual lives are the problem. They refuse to blame the badly listing ship itself.

When you view evangelicalism from a distance, it becomes clear that almost all the problems can be traced back to evangelicalism's unquestioned commitment to be successful and relevant. The demise of contemporary evangelical Christianity isn't happening because of liberals in Hollywood or Washington, D.C. but because of the misdirected brand of spirituality and community that is being promoted by the most successful evangelicals.

Let me repeat that. Many of those at the top of the pecking order—pastors and other leaders who are most sought after as experts on what Christianity is—are, in fact, the leading practitioners of religion that denies Jesus-shaped spirituality. Evangelicalism has become the sworn enemy of biblical Christianity. Instead, it's more like a fraternal lodge with its own language, rules, requirements, rituals, and secret handshake.

Like the ancient Hebrews, evangelicals are in the midst of a kind of exodus. It's a mass Jesus defection, a sweeping Jesus Disconnect that is sending former evangelicals to the ranks of nonbelief or toward other Christian options such as Roman Catholicism and Eastern Orthodoxy. For some, their rejection of the church will take them as far away as atheism. There are thousands of evangelicals who haven't been inside a church for years but still define themselves as a kind of evangelical. Like members of the peacetime National Guard, they are on inactive status.

Evangelical churches haven't lost a culture war or forgotten how to be relevant. They have become a movement that has so little to do with the centrality of Jesus that many people simply don't care any longer. And they aren't waiting around to see what's next. The people who don't accept the validity of the evangelical scorecard aren't tied in knots over activist judges or the latest outrage being shouted about on Christian talk radio. They are looking for authenticity, honesty, and spiritual integrity. Sadly, they won't find it in abundance in most churches.

Am I honestly saying that people are leaving Christianity behind because of a widespread and deeply affecting disconnect from Jesus? Yes.

Am I saying the church is at fault because it abandoned Jesus? Yes.

Am I saying the people who left the church are in the right? I'm saying I don't blame them at all.

LIKE PECAN PIE WITHOUT PECANS

Picture the most delicious pecan pie you ever had. The recipe came from Great-Grandma, and it has been passed down from generation to generation. That recipe for a "real" pecan pie is a living tradition in your family.

Go to any church potluck supper, and you'll see that a large number of excellent cooks make various claims to what it takes to get a pecan pie recipe right. Those cooks are the authorities, but everyone knows that different people expect different things from a pecan pie. You have your recipe, and I have mine. We can take them all to the county fair and have them judged, where even the judge has his or her own idea of what makes the best pecan pie.

But there is one thing no one would argue about, no matter what cookbook they use or which cook produced the pie. And it is this: the main ingredient in pecan pie is pecans. If we are disconnected from pecans, there is going to be a problem when we try to make pecan pie.

Now imagine—and I know this could be painful to those of you who know excellent pecan pie—a recipe that cuts the amount of pecans in half. Or a recipe that mixes pecans with other kinds of nuts. Even consider, if you can, the unthinkable: a pecan pie where pecans are entirely absent or only there occasionally in a random slice.

As bizarre as this may sound, I am sure you could find an expert who would stand behind a freshly baked, pecan-free pecan pie and commit culinary blasphemy by making a case for its superiority. "Some people don't really like pecans. Pecans can be hard to find in some parts of the country, and out of season they're expensive. Plus, they're hard to shell. Pecans are too fattening. These days, people want to try something new and different. Plus, did you hear about that new pastry shop outside Chicago that used a new recipe and sold thousands of pies?"

The relevance and authority of using pecans in pecan pie—according to the original recipe—will weaken as pie experts explain all the reasons for changing it. New versions of pecan pie will be a hit with all the right people who are interested in health, environmentalism, and culinary innovation. A fawning media will bring the attention of the masses to the new wave of pecan-free pecan pies. More than a few of the innovators will outright condemn the original recipe and its promoters as dangerous throwbacks to a time of fattening foods and high cholesterol.

Of course, if Great-Grandma were to be brought back from that glorious kitchen in the sky, and if she were able to look at the new, successful, brilliantly promoted pies of the present, she would have one profound comment: "That ain't no pecan pie." Folks, Great-Grandma would be right, no matter what the sales numbers said.

Jesus began a movement that was unapologetically about himself. One of his names in prophecy, Emmanuel, tells it all: "God with us." God was with us when Jesus came to be the One who rescued God's broken world.

Jesus gathered disciples and taught and enacted the Kingdom of God for three years. Jesus' message came to life in healings, exorcisms, raisings from the dead, miracles, parables, conversations, and stunning life transformations. Here was the Kingdom of God on earth: a transforming personal spirituality and a community that was shaped like Jesus himself.

And then Jesus was executed by the cruelty of an oppressive empire. The unimaginable reversal occurred as God paid the price for our rebellion and gave us his complete and undeserved acceptance. Jesus forgave his executioners and showed mercy to the thief dying with him. The sun hid its face, and all creation trembled. The spiritual realm reeled.

Jesus the God-man died, and hell enjoyed a brief triumph—brief because the Kingdom of God was coming alive in history's most stunning reversal: death conquered by resurrection life.

Jesus rose from three days of humiliation and seeming defeat. He regathered his followers and taught them again, this time with the Good News that nothing was ever going to be the same—not in the lives of those who believed, not in the world, not anywhere. The early Christians believed that Jesus had gone into the darkest places of the universe and announced life, freedom, and victory. Every enemy was defeated.

In the days to come, it was clear that Jesus did not want a continuing fan club or a franchise of temples and religious malls with his statue out front. No, he wanted a movement that would go into the whole world and point every person in every nation to himself. And so Jesus returned to heaven, sent the Holy Spirit to his followers, and empowered his movement to do what he had done, teach what he had taught, live as he had lived, and carry out what he had begun. From start to finish, it was a Jesus-shaped movement powered by the energy of the resurrected Lord himself.

THE CHURCH WITH VERY LITTLE OF JESUS

That's the recipe. Pecans. The real deal. I love 'em.

I've never met a Christian who didn't like that story of God sacrificing himself to save the rebellious mass of humanity who had chosen to reject him. I've never met anyone who would disagree with the importance of putting that Good News in the center of what it means to say you're a Jesus-follower. But when you start getting down to specifics, the pecans go quickly out the window.

If you don't believe me, have a seat and consider how Jesus got lost in the evangelical circus.

The largest church in the United States is pastored by a motivational speaker who tells his audiences how to improve their lives with a positive attitude and relentless efforts to be nice. His best-selling book tells readers how to have their best life now, with "the best" presented in unashamedly consumer-friendly, all-American terms. From getting a new house to finding a great parking space to simply being the one who always gets the goodies, this pastor leads millions of people every week to believe that Christianity is about you getting everything you want the way you like it so that you you you you...

At the end of his sermons, he encourages his hearers to "accept Jesus" into their hearts. Jesus is so insignificant in this presentation that his complete absence would make no difference. That one passing mention of Jesus is depressing; a small pecan for those who still want to believe Jesus is supposed to be involved in "church."

This pastor isn't alone. The message in thousands of evangelical churches is "God wants you to prosper." Which, in Western terms, means "God wants you to get rich." Whether it's the soft prosperity message of organizing your finances to get out of debt, the hard-core prosperity message of giving to God and getting back a hundredfold return, or the addictive hold that popular brand names have on the spending decisions of the average Christian, the message of offering material prosperity as the main business of Christianity is more popular than ever.

It's not just a desire for wealth that has corrupted evangelicalism. Sex is almost as exciting as cash. Pastor Ed Young Jr. of Dallas challenged the married couples in his church to have sex every day for seven days straight and then come to church to hear a sermon about the project. If right now you are admiring his assessment of congregational stamina, consider that Young was in the minor leagues compared to a Florida church that initiated a *forty-day* sex challenge.

I tuned into a program carried on the Trinity Broadcasting Network (TBN) and listened to a pastor and his wife preach about marital intimacy. As they talked to an audience, they were sitting on a bed. They weren't a particularly good-looking couple, by most standards, and their candor inspired disturbing mental imagery. I'm still a bit rattled.

And as to the subject of sex and how it relates to Jesus, who was a thoroughgoing celibate: yes, Jesus made it into all these sermons. If your Jesus isn't all about improving the frequency of your sex life, then it's time to trade up.

If money and sex don't do it for you, the church also supplies you with patriotism. A large church in Kentucky sponsors an annual "God and Country" rally at a baseball stadium. I've never attended the event, but the advertisements and news coverage make it clear that the God of the universe is in the business of blessing America in every single endeavor that involves war or the use of the military. I'm not talking about recognizing and honoring veterans. I'm saying that this pastor is swearing that

God is on our side no matter what, in every conflict, in every foreign-policy decision, and in every battle. Jesus doesn't just love America; Jesus is a flag-waving, gun-toting, pro-war conservative.

If you've read the four Gospels, or even just one of them, do you recall this guy? Jesus with a .44? Jesus wearing camo? Jesus reading *Soldier of Fortune*. Maybe it's like one old-time Baptist deacon in the segregated South who had this to say about integrating his congregation: "I don't care if God is for it; I'm agin' it."

So we've got money, sex, patriotism, and guns. That would do it for most of us, since we're inclined to greed, sensuousness, supporting the home team, and violence. But why stop there? The evangelical church seeks to serve everybody and their many interests, so it's not difficult to find Sunday-morning preaching that covers every topic imaginable while making no mention of Jesus at all.

It's not that evangelicals preach about Muhammad or Buddha or Krishna. It's more that they are interested in so many other things, like gays, the culture war, the coming election, gays, creeping socialism, how to raise better kids, how to beat stress, gays, and how many people got baptized last month. They also are intent on things such as vision, leadership, and destiny. Stop by any number of evangelical churches on Sunday morning, and you'll hear about all of these in terms that seldom mention Jesus and that totally miss what the Jesus movement is supposed to be about.

COMMUNITY OR COMPETITION?

And how about what passes for a sense of belonging and community in the evangelical world? Is it anything like the community Jesus gathered around himself? Is there evidence of scandalous inclusion? Does Sunday morning at First Evangelical Church look like the party the father threw for the returning prodigal, with feasting, singing, joy, and celebration because a dirty, smelly, foolish young man has come to his senses? Or does it look like a competition, a beauty pageant, an exercise in one-upmanship, like when the disciples said to Jesus, "Do for us whatever we ask of you"?[2]

Those disciples who requested this wanted to know which one of them would sit right next to Jesus in heaven. They wanted to bask in being his favorite. They wanted to be the guys who made it because the Guy they were with made it.

They were, like so many Christians, clueless about what Jesus was all about.

The Jesus Disconnect is everywhere. If you are still a passenger on the evangelical cruise liner, that lurching view of the iceberg isn't a wall mural. It's your ship heading to Davy Jones's locker. And if you are, like many of us, in a post-evangelical lifeboat putting distance between you and evangelical Christianity, you might have mixed feelings about losing something that could have been so real, authentic, and life changing. You are entitled to ask, how did this happen?

It's pecan pie without pecans, my friend.

Jesus saves. But as soon as that's out of the way, just hand the whole business back to us to run, and we'll call him when we have an emergency or if we need a guest appearance.

Is the prosperity message connected to Jesus?

Is the message of a great sex life, obedient and respectful kids, rising finances, great career, and a new house connected to Jesus?

Is the church-growth focus of the megachurch movement connected to the movement Jesus began and handed off to his followers?

As evangelical Christians find more ways to be successful and relevant in the eyes of American culture, are they remaining connected to Jesus? Or have they become experts at making pecan pie without pecans?

What If We're Wrong About God?

S o here's my idea.

I'd like to purchase a full-page ad in *Christianity Today, Charisma, Relevant,* and any other high-circulation Christian periodical willing to rent me the space. Then I want to air a fifteen-second spot at high noon on the ten biggest Christian radio stations and put a banner headline on the ten highest-traffic Christian Web sites.

Once I have the attention of the Christian world, I'd make an announcement: "I don't believe in God anymore."

Your response line is "What?"

Okay. I'm being provocative. Put down the phone and step back from your laptop. There's a little story here. In 2006 I had one of those years that made me wonder if I was actually a character in the mind of someone writing a B-grade movie about religious people finding out that— surprise!—all the stuff they believed God wouldn't ever let happen to them was going to happen anyway. As I worked through the rubble of my former certainties, I decided most of my pain was self-inflicted. I was toting around an idea of God that was torturing me.

In a moment of clarity, I told the people who were reading my blog that I was trading in my dysfunctional, religiously confused, magically programmed, stupidly self-centered idea of God for something more workable: Jesus. The "god I didn't believe in" was my set of accumulated ideas about what God was supposed to be doing to make life work the way I wanted. My unbelief was my announcement that I was giving up the old, defunct model of God for the God I had been talking about for years but not trusting or embracing in my life.

Saying "I don't believe in God...the god of my own ideas, concepts, and preferences" is a provocative way to restart the process of asking what faith is supposed to be in my life or in yours. That's risky business, especially for the Christians who want to have all the answers preprinted in red on a script you can pick up at any church. It's intimidating to consider the question, "What would it mean if we were wrong about God?"

Consider something with me, my fellow theological risk taker and provocateur: What if all this time, we've simply formed an idol in our mind, called it God, and worshiped it because it's more convenient and more comfortable that contending with a God who doesn't fit in a display case or make scheduled appearances at the religious mall? If exploring that question sounds interesting, then I'm going to invite you to grab that idol and haul it out to the curb for pickup.

It's easy for Christians to identify everyone else's idols. Hugh Hefner's bleached blondes, Bernie Madoff's crooked investment schemes, my neighbor's bass boat, the annoying bumper stickers that brag about the motorist's honor student. Christians have astoundingly clear vision when it comes to the vices, deceptions, and spiritual blindness of their neighbors. But when it comes to Sunday morning and what we hear from the pulpit and what gets talked about during the church coffee hour, it's another story.

Tell me what's worse: spending Sunday mornings at your cabin at the lake—fishing or sleeping late or reading the paper—or getting dressed up and going to church to worship the Creator of the universe, but mistaking him for an American, a celestial vending machine, or a ranting, red-faced radio-show host? One person who makes money or sex or power a false god is not a lot different from another person who concocts a god out of patriotism, sex, and money.

Wrong ideas about God are, themselves, false gods. They are idols just as much as a graven image. The god that smiles benignly and endorses my gradual submersion into the pursuit of the American dream needs to go. The god that inspires the culture of evangelical compromise has reached his expiration date. The gods of "big churches are better," "America is always right," "our sins are less sinful than their sins," "you have to look and sound like me to be acceptable"—they all need to go.

The false gods need to be replaced by the one true God who comes to us in the teachings, example, and power of Jesus of Nazareth. The short course in Christianity can be spelled out in a few words: Jesus is God. Lord and God. God revealing himself to human beings. The God-man. God in a bod. God in human flesh. God as a baby, a carpenter, a Jewish healer, a crucified falsely accused criminal, a risen conqueror, and a reigning King.[1]

My project to clean out my God closet and start over with the essentials leads me to Jesus Christ, God's ultimate and amazing self-description.

THE IMPORTANCE OF CHANGING YOUR MIND

When I was in seminary, I had a professor who was a brilliant theologian. His trademark statement in class was "Tear up your notes. I've changed my mind." I wasn't the only student who hoped I wasn't part of the unfortunate group that would discover that everything we'd learned the previous weeks as certain truth was no longer true at all.

I graduated without having to revisit and redefine everything I'd been taught, but later in life I discovered the value of that professor's words. The things you are certain of at age twenty-five lose a lot of luster by age forty, and even more by age fifty. As you follow God and hear from him and watch him work—and also watch him choose not to speak and act—the greater the chances that your early conception of him will be hidden in shadow. Over time, as you continue to follow God, you gain a humbler attitude about what you say about God. You also gain a desire for clarity and simplicity when you speak about God. When you are learning what Jesus means for your life and for the world, class is always in session. So hold your notes loosely, and keep the shredder handy.

Jesus' disciples catch a lot of flak for being dense and confused, even after Jesus tells them plainly what is about to happen to him. I have great sympathy for those fishermen. Jesus never said, "I've changed my mind. Tear up your notes." But being Jesus' student had to be a volatile experience of constant worldview explosion. A lot of notes, previous answers, cultural assumptions, and learned presumptions were going into the trash can every day.

Have you always believed it's wrong to touch a leper? Tear up your notes.

How about the strict rules that forbid speaking to a woman in public or allowing her to touch you? Tear up your notes.

Do you think you know how to pray? Tear up your notes.

Are you certain you know who God is punishing and rewarding? You might want to check again.

You thought you were clear on God's attitude toward the Roman occupiers and other Gentiles? Jews are not allowed to eat with them, or go into their homes, or accept them as being righteous unless they became Jews. Right? Sorry, you can throw that notebook away.

Do you understand whom God loves and includes? Whom God dislikes and ignores? Do you know who is in and who's out of God's Kingdom? Who is great in God's Kingdom? The answers, as Jesus gave them, bear little resemblance to what the right-thinking Jews of that day were convinced was true, based on what they'd been taught. Then Jesus came along, claiming to be God, but he had most of the old Jewish traditions and teachings all wrong.

Or so it must have seemed to his disciples.

THINKING YOU REALLY KNOW GOD

By the time Jesus came to earth, the Jews had already known God for thousands of years. They had seen God create them as a mighty nation from a childless pagan named Abraham. God had taken care of them through good times and bad, even going to the trouble of rescuing them out of slavery in Egypt to preserve them as a people. He gave them their own homeland and defeated their enemies. The Jews knew all about heavy religious subjects such as redemption, blood sacrifice, the necessity of the blameless paying the blood price for those worthy of blame. They knew all about forgiveness and salvation. They had received ten commandments directly from God; they were the world's first people to insist there was only one creator God. They knew the truth about God, and they repeated the biggest stories about God and his actions to their children every year during their most important religious observance— Passover.

Then a Man arrived who claimed to be the King whom the nation of Israel had been waiting on for centuries. First-century Jews knew exactly what a king, especially a King sent from God, was supposed to do: destroy Israel's enemies, rescue the nation from humiliation, clean up politics and religion, and bring the Kingdom of God. Quite a list, and every Jew in every village knew the Messiah's job description.

And, of course, all of this was familiar to Jesus' disciples. These are the same disciples whose detailed notes on what it looks like to be the Messiah Jesus sent to the shredder.

Imagine you're Matthew or John or James or Peter. You're familiar with the Passover meal your people have been celebrating for more than a thousand years. The one that commemorates the Jews' deliverance from Egypt. Well, Jesus says, "I've got a new explanation to give you, and I think you're going to be surprised." He then explained that there was a new Lamb in town, and animal sacrifices at the temple were no longer sufficient to atone for the people's sins. "Someone else's blood is going to save you: mine."

The truth, as the disciples had been taught all their lives, suddenly was recast and fulfilled by a Man who acted like God and reversed every expectation these men had always had of what God was supposed to be like.

Peter, James, John, and the other disciples weren't theologians, but they understood the religion of synagogue, law, and temple; depended on the sacrificial system; and trusted the biblical interpretations of the rabbis. But after three years with Jesus, their view of God, his Kingdom, his Messiah, their future, and what it meant to be a person living in God's world was turned upside down like the tables of the money-changers. Jesus wouldn't leave their ideas of God alone until he was their idea of God.

When I read the gospel of John in particular, I can imagine what a wild ride it must have been to be around Jesus. People who loved God and sought to obey him found their deepest beliefs about God were suddenly revolutionized by what they experienced with Jesus. Old certainties vanished. Undeniable new realities appeared and changed everything.

"Before Abraham was, I am."

"You search the Scriptures…. But the Scriptures point to me!"

"Unless you eat the flesh of the Son of Man and drink his blood, you have no life in you."

"Which one of you convicts me of sin?"

"I and the Father are one."

"I am the resurrection and the life."

"I'm the only One who knows the Father; and you'll only know him if you know me."

"If you've seen and heard me, you've seen and heard God."[2]

Being a disciple of Jesus meant you had joined a demolition party aimed at everything you'd ever believed about God. There must have been nightly meetings when Jesus wasn't around, when the disciples tried to process the impossible concept Jesus had introduced that day. It took a certain kind of faithful Jew to hang around a radical Rabbi who insisted on teaching his own unorthodox take on the law and the prophets every day. And that doesn't even begin to address the blasphemy of claiming equality with God. What was a Jewish fisherman or tax collector to do with something like that?

I'm surprised a few of the disciples, or most of them, didn't jump ship. And why didn't they?

"Where else can we go? He has the words of eternal life"[3] must have been a frequent conclusion.

For the disciples, being a Jesus-follower was the life of a man who enlisted in an ongoing God revolution. A Jesus-shaped truth invasion broke into that safe place where they used to keep their long-held ideas about God. Like a tornado, Jesus blew their ideas and concepts into splinters and dust. What was left?

Jesus. The Tornado himself. "Whoever has seen me has seen the Father."[4] If that doesn't blow away your personally decorated religious playroom, I don't know what will.

It's hard to appreciate how difficult it was for the disciples to stick with Jesus during those days when he was redefining everything they'd been taught. We tend to think of the courage it took to proclaim Jesus as the Savior after he rose from the dead. We often overlook the inner conflicts the disciples would have faced before Jesus was crucified, when he was strong and healthy and walking around Judea and Galilee, teaching and performing miracles, and causing a scandal just about everywhere he went.

The disciples had to discard more false notions, incomplete teachings, erroneous assumptions, and long-held absolutes in three years than most of us will in a lifetime. But if we are followers of Jesus, as they were, then shouldn't we be forced to reevaluate these same things in our lives and in our thinking? If this was the experience of the disciples, why isn't it the experience of more of us who call ourselves followers and believers today?

THE FACE OF A DISCIPLE

My students and family know that my emotions are instantly readable in my facial expression. If I'm happy, I can't avoid smiling or tearing up. If I'm angry, my face shows it. I notice the same thing about other people. When I think of the disciples, I can see their faces as Jesus goes about his mission. Their faces tell a story.

Look at their faces as Jesus is talking with a despised, immoral, Samaritan woman. Look at them as he commands them to love their enemies. Look at their faces as he says they must become like children if they want to be God's children. Notice their expressions when he tells them that the rich have a very difficult path into the Kingdom of Heaven. Look at their faces as Jesus forgives the sin of a paralyzed man or eats with a prostitute, says he'll replace the sacred temple or calls a hated tax collector to be his student.

Look at their faces as calm air replaces a raging storm, as demon-possessed pigs pile over one another into the ocean, as a four-days-dead Lazarus stumbles out of the grave, or as Jesus takes over the temple courts, saying, "This is my house!"

Look at their faces as their Rabbi turns their familiar Passover into a prophecy and a remembrance of his own murder. Look at them as he refuses to use his power to resist arrest, as he tells them in advance that he will go to Jerusalem, be rejected by his own people, be executed unjustly on a cross, and that three days later, he will be raised from the dead…and then does exactly that.

Look at their faces as he says, "The universe is mine, and you are to tell the Roman Empire and the rest of the world about me, my Kingdom, and my salvation."[5]

I think their faces would tell us they were utterly blown away, all the time, from A to Z and beyond, by this astonishing God-man, Jesus. The disciples expressed it succinctly on one occasion: "Who is this man?"[6] Their inherited, accepted, and approved ideas about God were being demolished and replaced, not by new ideas, but by a carpenter from Nazareth who was convincing them he was the Lord God.

The passionate message of the gospel is to abandon all hope in any other god, god-substitute, or god-replacement. Instead, Jesus-followers live in a world where they are deeply, stubbornly loyal to the one God they know through the One who uniquely shows us what God is like.

> Therefore, as to the eating of food offered to idols, we know
> that "an idol has no real existence," and that "there is no God
> but one." For although there may be so-called gods in heaven
> or on earth—as indeed there are many "gods" and many
> "lords"—yet for us there is one God, the Father, from whom
> are all things and for whom we exist, and one Lord, Jesus
> Christ, through whom are all things and through whom we
> exist.[7]

For us there is one God, and he is recognizable as the One who came to us in Bethlehem, walked the roads of Galilee, died as a criminal on the cross, and rose from death on Easter. Our one God has spoken so we can know him and his Word to us: *Jesus.*

REMOVE, REPENT, RENEW, REFORM

It goes without saying that as Jesus-followers we have been given a mission to remove all idols, repent, renew our minds, and reform our lives. We should be wearing signs: Beware! Ongoing Theological Deconstruction and Construction Zone!

That Christ-following teacher Paul stated the goal of a Jesus-shaped faith journey perfectly:

> For though we walk in the flesh, we are not waging war according to the flesh. For the weapons of our warfare are not of the flesh but have divine power to destroy strongholds. We destroy arguments and every lofty opinion raised against the knowledge of God, and take every thought captive to obey Christ.[8]

I will assume that most of us have not found our experience with Christianity to be this intensely and completely Jesus centered. While I've heard a preacher talk about taking every thought captive to obey Jesus, while he waves around a Bible and sounds completely serious, the reality has been a bit different. We are told to obey Jesus, but the standard of conduct and the leading characteristics of a faithful Christian life curiously avoid Jesus. It's almost as if there is an unspoken agreement that it's unfair to bring Jesus in as the definition and measurement of following Jesus.

When I first began to think about Jesus-shaped spirituality, I would ask this door-opening question: If I spent three years with Jesus, how would I feel about…? The question is appropriate and revealing, no matter what the subject or issue happens to be. How would Jesus shape me in this area if he deeply influenced my thinking and living?

While I obviously couldn't answer that question perfectly, it pointed me in the right direction, which is a close examination of what it means to take Jesus seriously. If Jesus himself is the complete picture of what it looks like to follow Jesus, then what should the Christian life look like?

I actually liked the WWJD bracelets. Not so much as bracelets, but as a kind of acid test for whatever project is under consideration, from premarital sex to building a $70 million "sanctuary." Put any decision, contemplated action, or words you're about to utter to the test of what would Jesus do.

I was surprised to find that a lot of teachers and preachers thought that "What would Jesus do?" was a flawed idea. They preferred something like "What does the church teach?" or "What does the Bible, rightly interpreted, teach?" Or maybe "What does this mean for Christians today?" Others were simply cynical that Christians would ever know enough about Jesus to answer the question.

I wonder if it strikes anyone as strange that Christians often adopt a system where we know that Jesus wouldn't do the thing we are considering, but we feel free to do it anyway. Would Jesus drive a Lexus? For many Christians, it doesn't seem to matter. I'm convinced that Jesus wouldn't wear a $5,000 wristwatch or drive an $80,000 car. And no one I know believes he would build a $70 million worship center. But all of that gets set aside. We can arrive at our own decision, dismiss what Jesus would do, and go ahead and do what we want.

FOLLOWING JESUS HAS TO LOOK LIKE JESUS

As we think about following Jesus by actually thinking about Jesus, things take an unexpected turn. We find that we have to reject a type of cynicism that is prevalent among Christians. The assumption is that even if we fully understood the "Jesus way of life," we could never live that way. The result is that Christians live on easy autopilot, where the standard shifts from living like Jesus to "being a good Christian." The guiding principles are to avoid rocking the boat, to be nice, and to fit in. Does it seem to anyone else that the autopilot Christian life is primarily about how to get a reserved seat on the flight to heaven, assure yourself a nice trip, and look forward to a smooth landing?

But following Jesus leads to an entirely different kind of life. My experience is this: Jesus shakes me up, and I can't get it together very well on my own. I absolutely do not have my head or heart wrapped around all the implications of Jesus' life and teachings. I can't understand Jesus on my own, and I certainly can't sustain this journey alone. When I get into the four Gospels and consider the meaning of Jesus' gospel message, I see myself and my spirituality differently. Suddenly I feel like I've completely missed the point. I've been formed by the lukewarm church at Laodicea (the one that made Jesus want to vomit) and not by the bold and countercultural church at Smyrna.[9]

There's no way to keep going on this adventure of making Jesus my only Lord and God without the community of Jesus around me, attempting the same project. None of us can do this alone.

What I need is a personal transformation by the real Christ, not the one that is manufactured by organized Christianity. I need to be changed by the Jesus who never agrees to be quiet and cooperative. I also need a movement of culture-resisting, church-suspicious rebels and Jesus-followers who have taken the same view of religion that Jesus took in his scorching denouncements of religious phoniness.[10]

I'm swimming in a sea of mediocrity, worshiping in a church captivated by consumerism, and deeply affected by a skewed view of God that the Bible would call petty idolatry. My life frequently sucks, and I sometimes wonder why Jesus doesn't send me a note asking whose holy book I've been reading. I need a ragtag family of Jesus-shaped disciples to pull me out when I'm floundering and teach me how to swim with the Lord of the universe in these putrid and dangerous cultural waters.

I need to read and hear the Bible taught with the passionate integrity of Jesus, not the manipulation and misrepresentation of modern Christianity-lite. I need a commitment to the Bible that is unapologetically Jesus centered. I don't need to hear about a magic book of life principles for suburban success.

I need some truthful talk—not safely scripted chitchat—about what it means to follow Jesus. I want a place where I am allowed to raise my questions and verbalize my struggles, a place where I can mess up and be prayed for, and I want to be able to stumble and still be accepted on the team. I need to see and know real human beings who have walked the path of hard choices and hard times in order to remain faithful to Jesus.

I need a cadre of friends who pray like Jesus, who step across the lines to include outcasts, and who open the Lord's Table to those Jesus invited to that table. I need fellow students who hold the ancient faith of the church in their minds and the mission of Jesus in their hearts.

I don't need this community to try to replace Jesus or to promise to dispense Jesus like a product. I don't need leaders who think they are above me or who worship at the altar of celebrity. I don't need a contrived experience, but a fellowship and a family. I simply need brothers and sisters who will start me on the journey, encourage me along the way, and keep the map right there where I can see it and we can talk about it.

If I'm going to trade my false gods for the great God and Savior, Jesus Christ, I need the help of a radically Jesus-shaped community. I need companions and teachers who will not remain silent about what Jesus said about money; who won't ignore his words on servant leadership; who agree with Jesus about the church's mission; and who won't edit, translate, and reshape Jesus into an enabler of conformity.

I need to know I'm not alone in the quest for a Jesus-shaped spirituality. This isn't the shortcut, and it's not the easy way. Jesus does not make the Christian life simple. He's not a mood-altering pill or a purveyor of instant bliss. I realize this life is going to be a long journey, so I need friends who won't give up.

I believe Jesus. I certainly believe in him, but that is the easier part for me. Believing all Jesus says and commands can be tough, but I believe Jesus when he says he has my life and will give it to me in the process of my being a disciple:

And calling the crowd to him with his disciples, he said to them, "If anyone would come after me, let him deny himself and take up his cross and follow me. For whoever would save his life will lose it, but whoever loses his life for my sake and the gospel's will save it. For what does it profit a man to gain the whole world and forfeit his soul? For what can a man give in return for his soul?[11]

Jesus is my God. He's the image of the invisible; the spoken Word of the silent and enigmatic One. He's the answer to the mysteries of "who are we?" and "why am I here?"

Jesus is a life-altering Word. To hear him, know him, and believe him is to come into a new world while I still have both feet firmly planted in this one.

That's why I need you, if you are one of the people determined to lose every other god and worship the only One, Jesus. I need you if you are done with your own ideas about God and are weary of academic theological speculations about God. If, like the first disciples, your life is an ongoing demonstration of what happens when Jesus is accepted at face value, I need you on my team.

It may continue to shock people when I say I don't believe in the god I used to believe in and when I encourage others to clean out the falsehoods and cultural garbage that has accumulated in their own ideas of God. It may still shake up a few Christians when I admit that following Jesus makes me feel like a beginner every day and a failure most days. But these honest admissions lead toward the essentials of discipleship and genuine relationships with real Jesus-followers. Every day that we come to Jesus and every day that we journey with his friends and followers, we're starting over with great grace. The Good News of a new life, a new world, and a new hope for everyone isn't the arrival of easy answers. It's the end of every answer but Jesus, and the discovery that all we are and ever hope to be is a treasure buried in a field...a treasure we recognize in a crucified carpenter who happens to be the Son of God.

A Christianity
Jesus Would Recognize

Words, particularly religious words, are interesting things. Most conservative religious people are loyal to a familiar vocabulary. Start using words they don't know, and you'll be put on close-observation status so they can check you for heresy.

I'm on good terms with the major dialect of my Southern Baptist upbringing. I know what it means to get saved, come to the altar, rededicate my life, surrender to preach, pray through, and put out a fleece. I also know advanced terms like *revival meeting, soul winner, intermediate department*, and *watch night*.

If you go to my people and say, "We're going to have a special," they smile, and it's not because they think you're buying them drinks or food. They think you're there to sing to them, as in "Brother Norm will now bring special music." If, however, you say "Jesus-shaped spirituality," they will not smile and they will ask you to produce a signed baptism certificate. You, brother or sister, are now suspect.

Further, I'm aware that trendy, goatee-wearing, Starbucks-sipping, preaching-from-a-couch neohippies in the "emerging" church love to crank out novel terms as substitutes for the shopworn lexicon of the traditional church. I'm still enough of a Baptist that it annoys me when someone says "holistic" or "cohort" in a sermon.

I realize that my using a phrase such as *Jesus-shaped spirituality* will send a signal to some that I have a soul patch, a hemp man-purse, and a

David Crowder hairstyle. (Extremely wrong on all three, by the way. Especially the hair.) To others, my insistence on pushing Jesus-shaped spirituality will signal that I have abandoned Bible-believing Christianity and become a liberal, a compromiser, and a social-gospel nut. Also not true.

You need to know that I wouldn't haul out this little phrase if I didn't believe it would pay off in our greater understanding of Jesus. I'm not just playing with words. I didn't coin the phrase to impress anyone, nor did I come up with it in hopes I'd be invited to speak at a hip conference called "Fuel" or some such.

I tell my students that "vocabulary is education," and I believe it. As we learn to think with new words and communicate in new ways, we grow in our understanding of the world and our place in it. Anyone can know God in a vague sense, but when we embrace words such as *justification* and *covenant,* our appreciation of God grows.

WHAT IS JESUS-SHAPED SPIRITUALITY?

Jesus-shaped spirituality is a way to talk about three things that deeply matter, even to people outside the church:

1. Jesus
2. Having a genuine experience of God
3. Figuring out how a life gets transformed

I've talked with hundreds of people who have left the church or who desperately want to but are held back by family, paycheck, tradition, expectations, or the threadbare hope that things will change for the better. No matter what their experience with organized Christianity, they have not abandoned all belief. Even for those who have left the church, for the most part they still believe...

- That if there is someone who is the clue, the meaning, and the key to the deepest questions of life, it will almost certainly be Jesus. Jesus remains, despite two millennia of rotten publicity from his followers, a universally attractive and compelling Person.

- That if God is out there, then to know and experience God's presence, kindness, love, and goodness would be this life's greatest gift.
- That just because the church promised meaning and truth but failed to deliver it, that is no reason to become hopelessly cynical about God.

Give this a try sometime: talk to any random sample of the human population, from active church members to ex-church members to Mormons and Muslims and others. To a person, you will find that life transformation matters, and Jesus is still high on the list of those who are capable of showing you how to pull it off.

I have chosen to speak and write about Jesus-shaped spirituality to help people stop being sabotaged by religion and start thinking about Jesus again. Few things are more boring or off-putting than talking about the church. No matter what your experience of organized religion has been—positive, negative, or indifferent—we can easily find something to disagree about when we start comparing churches. It's a waste of time.

But how people inside and outside of the church think about Jesus, now that's another subject entirely. Which is why I'm doing my best to continually press Jesus as the center of the conversation. For too long, the people who characterize themselves as followers of Jesus have been making pecan pie but leaving out the pecans. The Jesus Disconnect is everywhere. I want everyone to feel the creative tension that arises when we bring Jesus back and put him in the spotlight. Jesus himself, not formulations of Christian doctrine or church traditions, will transform our faith, lives, and relationships. You can't have a Christian experience, in a church or outside one, without Jesus.

YOU CAN'T CONTROL JESUS

I'm a classroom teacher much of the time, and one of my biggest challenges is the student who wants to run the show. At least once a year, I'll get a student who assumes he or she is in charge of the class. Or should be. These students stand when the class sits, they talk when they should listen, and they declare themselves an exception from every rule and expectation. I'll explain what the class needs to do, and they will grin and do as they please.

Most of these students aren't really hostile. They simply lost, somewhere along the way, the simple truth that they aren't in control.

Our big problem with Jesus is that we want to control things, and he turns out to be remarkably difficult to control. In the Christian enterprise, we like to formulate definitions, establish norms, and set parameters for acceptable experiences. We have empowered ourselves to determine what is and is not an appropriate relationship with Jesus, based on how we think Christianity should look and work. And according to the church's routine definitions, Jesus is all-accepting of our particular approach to spirituality.

Remember my earlier Jesus-shaped question, If I were to spend three years with Jesus, what kind of person would I be? The reaction I get from most people, when I put this question to them, is astonishingly backward from what you might expect. Instead of arguing about possible answers to how Jesus would treat women or what Jesus thought about multimillion-dollar buildings, the question itself comes under suspicion. They turn the question around: Why are you asking this? Is this really something that should concern us as good Christians?

I have said this before: most Christians are not comfortable with the idea that Jesus should be allowed to define our beliefs, lifestyle, preferences, priorities, faith, values, actions, and spirituality. Like the control-oriented student who explains that my ideas for running the class really don't apply to him, Christians have invented a spirituality that has Jesus on the cover but not in the book.

Here's a simple example. Think about yourself if you had just spent three years with Jesus. How would you treat illegal immigrants? For vast numbers of typical American Christians, their immediate instincts are to either argue a political position or look for a way to end the conversation.

"What does Jesus have to do with illegal immigrants?" an uncomfortable Christian might ask. "That's for the politicians to decide." Or a person might ponder, "What does my favorite radio talk-show host say about this?" Or she might try to research the position that is held by a leading Christian she's heard about: "The Christian bookstore didn't have a book on this topic, but they had a special on Precious Moments figurines."

If the person should resort to the Bible, he almost certainly will hunt for a verse in the Old Testament, not a passage from the Gospels. "That's really not something Jesus had anything to say about. Doesn't the Old Testament say something about being gracious and generous to those who are aliens and foreigners?"

And then there is the concerned, evangelistic answer: "I'll just say that if the church runs across any illegals, we should try to evangelize them."

Every one of these sidesteps the real issue. Some of the answers could be better, and some could be a lot worse, but it's the process of how we consider the issues that matters to me. Jesus talked about a lot of things, but not everything. In many cases, his actions spoke for him. In other cases, what he failed to do spoke volumes about what he wanted his followers to be like.

So where do we look for the key to a Jesus-shaped answer to questions related to immigration or economic opportunity or housing or fighting poverty? Well…how about looking at Jesus?

Jesus was an expert on including those who were officially excluded. He knew all about illegals, at least as far as first-century Judaism was concerned.

His personal outreach to the people whom religion officially avoided was one of the most distinctive and shocking things about Jesus. Here was the Jewish Messiah who kept thumbing his nose at hundreds of years of Jewish tradition, religious authority, and unquestioned codes of behavior. He kept tearing down rules and traditions by saying hated Samaritans were okay and despised tax collectors were loved by God.

Whether it was Jesus befriending hookers, talking to Romans in public, or healing lepers without the express written permission of the temple authorities, Jesus knew all about showing that the Kingdom of God includes outsiders. Peter, who spent three years with Jesus, called Christians "aliens."[1] We are living on earth, where in an eternal sense we don't belong. We are temporarily living away from home, having been displaced from paradise.

As aliens and strangers on earth, we shouldn't ask how Jesus would treat illegal immigrants and stop there. We should figure out how to live in the world as "aliens," which Peter declares us to be. And we should realize that we can learn much from the outsiders whom Jesus included.

Jesus' teachings make it clear that the banquet to be held at the end of the present age will be well attended by those who are widely considered to be rejects and undesirables. What does the Kingdom of God look like? It's well stocked with illegal aliens given dignity, acceptance, and identity by Jesus.

If you are a Christian, not only are you away from home, but you are living in a foreign culture. God's Kingdom is not the kingdom of the world, so as a Jesus-follower you are living in an earthly culture where you don't belong. That's one reason why it doesn't matter to me if you are a Rush Limbaugh acolyte or president of the Al Franken Fan Club. The mission for a Jesus-shaped person and a Jesus-influenced movement would be the same when it comes to illegal immigrants: at whatever tables you preside over, include the excluded. Jesus does. If you follow him, so do you. In fact, if you follow him, you are one yourself.

However, this isn't how most American Christians think. American Christians gravitate to those who agree with them and are most welcoming toward those who swear allegiance to the church-approved doctrines and practices. Most Christians prefer to spend time with those who mirror themselves, which happens because Jesus isn't in charge of the class. The students have taken over and replaced Jesus' way of life with their own preferences. Jesus has become an impediment, a complicating factor to doing what we want.

If you doubt this, give the following some thought. We have decided that Jesus can't sit in judgment of our politics, our choices, our exercise of power, or our relationships. Deep down, we don't want to see his prayer answered, "on earth as it is in heaven."[2] For a number of reasons, we don't want Jesus to create a present moment where the Kingdom of God takes shape on earth. Instead, our refashioned version of Jesus removes Jesus from the stage and silences his influence. This frees us to allow political pundits, shock jocks, and culture warriors to tell us what to do. We have found that it's far more comfortable to adopt their opinions as our own.

EXAMPLES OF CHRISTIAN JESUS-AVERSION

Lest you think I'm overstating my case, let me illustrate. I have noticed an undeniable "Jesus aversion" in many quarters of the church. At a recent conference, I heard one of America's most popular pastors—a staunch conservative who was holding a large Bible in his hands—say we need to preach and teach about the ascended, reigning Christ and avoid teaching and preaching Jesus as he lived during his earthly ministry. Too intense a focus on the Jesus who lived on earth, according to this preacher, will reduce Jesus to an example and will influence Christians away from the gospel.

In other words: Give people Jesus in heaven, because if you talk about the Guy running around in the Gospels, you are going to wind up being a heretic. Fixing people's attention on Jesus as he comes across in the incarnation will distract them from the truth.

Let's look more deeply into this bizarre Jesus-aversion.

There is a school of thought among many Christians that Jesus was sloppy in his theology. They aren't saying he was wrong, just that he was not as comprehensive or systematic as a really helpful Christian like John Calvin. This view sets up a strange conflict between Jesus and just about everyone in church history. The Christians who caution us not to base too much of our theology on Jesus aren't arguing that Jesus is in error, but that he often is unclear, paradoxical, inconvenient, impractical, and off topic. Watching Christians find ways to wrestle a huge, central idea of Scripture such as the Kingdom of God off the table and into the closet is an ugly scene. And the results of negating Jesus' teachings on the Kingdom open the door to all manner of unfortunate, man-made churchianity.

When I talk about the need for a Jesus-shaped faith, life, belief, or spirituality, I'm trying to call attention to an issue that is turning Christianity into something that deserves to be walked out on. I want to create the tension we have been avoiding. I want to empower you to ask the questions that the current crop of pastors and other church leaders have designated as irrelevant.

Would Jesus recognize the church of twenty-first-century North America as the movement he began? I'm not interested in how the youth program introduces people to Jesus or how the Easter pageant presented the last days of Christ. I want to know what would happen if Jesus paid a quality-control visit. Would he recognize this movement, as we've reconstructed it, as bearing any resemblance to what he began in those forty days post-resurrection and beyond?

Does what we say resemble what Jesus said? With four Gospels to work with, the words and teachings of Jesus are not hard to find. If Christians really do believe what Jesus said, do we sound anything like him? Do books written by Christians sound anything like Jesus' appearances in the

Gospels? Did he even once mention our need to receive him as our personal Savior? Did he constantly talk about "discovering your destiny through your dreams"? Was church growth a major Jesus topic? If not, why not? And where did we come up with all the things we love to devote conferences to?

Does the church's version of discipleship look like what Jesus did with his disciples? From reading the Gospels, we know how and where Jesus called his disciples. We know what he taught them. We know where he took them. We know what they spent their time doing. We know what he released them to do on their own. We know his frustrations, as well as their questions and the failures and conflicts they encountered. We know what Jesus did to develop them into apostolic leaders. We should be able to answer the question, Are we producing Jesus-shaped, Jesus-formed, and Jesus-transformed people?

THE NORTH-AMERICAN JESUS

Christians used to sing about imitating Christ and becoming a version of Jesus others could see and read. That sentiment assumes we have some idea what Jesus is like. But what if we really don't have much idea at all what Jesus is like? What if our actual song is "Just look at me, and call it Jesus"?

Picture a time in organized Christianity when Christians have decided to pursue their own ideas of what it means to be religious and then announce that this is what Jesus was really like. Christians might decide the godly thing to do is to isolate themselves from outsiders, to protect believers from the vast population of "unacceptables," to make spirituality another form of consumerism, and to agree to excuse the list of acceptable sins. Christians could do this and at the same time insist they were presenting a credible witness to Jesus of Nazareth.

I've seen it done that way. In fact, I see it being done almost every day. Christians have pushed Jesus aside and replaced his plain teachings with patriotism, nationalism, denominationalism, entertainment, and their personal desires to live comfy in the culture.

Christians say they are followers of Jesus, but are they more accurately occasional fans of Jesus? Maybe once a week? If someone wanted to know the way of Jesus, the values of Jesus, and the practices of Jesus, would observing the life of an American Christian give them accurate information? Do Jesus' most direct words on discipleship shape the way we live?

As a person who communicates for a living, I know the frustration of having my words turned into something I never meant. So imagine how Jesus would react to Christians recasting his words into the AEV, the American Evangelical Version of the Bible:

- The Sermon on the Mount doesn't apply to any of us today. It's for the Millennium, which won't arrive anytime soon.
- The Sermon on the Mount is a collection of spiritual principles that, when properly interpreted, mean something completely different from what they seem to say. So chill.
- The Sermon on the Mount is legalistic. If you teach people to actually do what it says, you are abandoning grace for law.
- Most of Jesus' teaching was directed at the original apostles. You weren't one of them, so it's not for you.
- If you want to know what Jesus really means, read Paul's letters, not the Gospels.
- If you want to know the details of what Jesus means, read our church's doctrinal statement.
- If you want to know what Jesus means in the context of today, our pastor has a new sermon series out on DVD.
- Jesus saves, but after that the Holy Spirit will tell you what to do.
- Jesus' difficult sayings are figurative. You shouldn't try to take him literally.

IF YOU ARE A LEAVER, OR WANT TO BE ONE

If you have already left the church or are about to, what does all this have to do with you? Primarily this: I seriously doubt that what you are walking away from resembles the movement Jesus started, the process Jesus used to produce disciples, or a serious engagement with the teaching and example of Jesus. I would guess that what you walked away from bears a superficial resemblance to the way of Jesus. I also would expect that what you left behind bears more than a passing resemblance to one of the religious systems that Jesus repudiated.

For many of you, leaving the church may have been the most spiritually healthy thing you ever did.

In the early 1990s, rock vocalist Jackson Browne penned a Christmas song for the Irish band the Chieftains. Both artists recorded the tune, but the song took on a life of its own quite separate from the Christmas holiday. That song, "The Rebel Jesus," isn't really a Christmas song at all, but an extraordinary poem suggesting that those who most frequently sing about and celebrate Jesus may, in fact, have chosen to neuter his edginess and abandon his bold mission. Could it be, Browne asks, that the great celebration of Christ's birth is quite far from the spirit and passionate center of the heart and vision of Jesus himself?

Browne has never claimed to be a Christian, but like many of those outside the church, he knows something about Jesus. He suspects that the advertised, official Jesus franchise with the large sign and the nice, happy crowd may not be remotely on track with Jesus. Browne understands, in part, what it means to be Jesus-shaped. It means living a life that points to Jesus and doesn't deceive the world about what Jesus is like.

If a self-described "heathen and pagan" such as Jackson Browne can see the truth, why can't those who claim to follow Christ see it?[3] It's a matter of spirituality, and that's where we're going next.

What Does Jesus-Shaped Spirituality Mean?

The effect of the word *spirituality* on Christians is a mysterious thing to observe. It is no exaggeration to say that if I know your response to the word *spirituality,* I can tell you at least twenty other things about yourself that you've never told me. I know, for instance, whom you voted for in the last presidential election, your favorite television news network, and where your kids are being educated.

Spirituality has become a code word in the constantly evolving carnival of Christian jargon. For traditional, conservative church folk, spirituality is a strange intruder into the Christian vocabulary. Billy Graham never said it, at least not in public. If your pastor said it, he wasn't smiling at the time. He was most likely talking about the spiritual deception that emerges from people such as Oprah Winfrey or that guy who wrote *Blue Like Jazz.*

On the other hand, if you come from more mainline Protestant stock, *spirituality* is a perfectly good Christian word. The fact that your church sponsors classes on spirituality doesn't give anyone a heart attack. It's an acceptable, even popular, way to refer to personal faith without constant reference to the institutional church and its battles over orthodoxy. Mainline Christians insist that Christian spirituality is exactly what Jesus was teaching.

I realize that my using the expression *Jesus-shaped spirituality* as a way to recalibrate the Christian message runs the risk of sliding into the Christian-terminology sinkhole and never coming out. As with most things in the alternate world of Christian culture, my personal sympathies are firmly planted on both sides of this divide. You have to be careful where you point that spirituality thing, because it has the potential to grant legitimacy to all kinds of people who have nothing more interesting to say than "worship yourself." On the other hand, if the pursuit of spirituality gets us away from the problems so many people have with the church and allows us to talk about our experience of God and where it comes from, I'm all for it.

So if you are a person who gave up talking about God and religion because it was such a frustrating dead end, I'll admit to slipping *spirituality* in there as an incentive to get you back into the conversation. (Or perhaps you just opened your concordance next to your *ESV Study Bible,* and you didn't find the word *spirituality* anywhere in the Bible. I realize that's the case. Of course, neither will you find *complementarianism, quiet time, purity vow, traditional values, Second Amendment,* or *just war.*

But I understand the concern over a word, such as *spirituality,* that is used freely by those who claim no faith whatsoever in the Judeo-Christian God. So we'll be watching our step as we go.

I'm taking the position that the term *spirituality* is useful to the extent that it helps us talk about Jesus and ourselves with clearer understanding. Meanwhile, to the extent it puts Jesus on the same level with the guy selling ShamWow, I accept the caution light. All I ask is this: let's use this term to help us take a fresh look at Jesus. Instead of assuming that what we're already doing always produces an accurate reflection of Jesus, let's ask what Jesus himself was seeking to produce as he lived and taught.

THE THINGS THAT SHAPE US

Some people look like their dogs. I don't understand this phenomenon, but I've observed it too often to deny it. Maybe people subconsciously want to own a dog that looks like a relative. Big and shaggy, or small and hyper.

Other people look like what they eat. You know how that works, especially those of you who love giant burritos at midnight.

I'm sure there's a Web page somewhere featuring people who look like their cars. I'll leave that as a complete mystery.

Invest yourself in anything, from watching *South Park* to obsessing over your lawn, and it will alter what kind of person you are. Human beings aren't static, but dynamic. We change. We are influenced, nurtured, moved, and moldable. While there are limits to how much anyone can or will change, we share a common trait of being uniquely shaped by the influences and relationships that touch our lives.

If humans are spiritual by nature, and if we were created to relate to God, then our lives will bear the imprint of that interaction. And so…it's essential that we talk about and understand spirituality.

The starting point of spiritual experience is as basic as breathing. All humans have some sort of personal experience of God by virtue of being human beings. God created us (let's hold the debate for later) and gave us his image as a gift. In a mysterious yet essential way, you have the imprint of God on you.[1] God built into you a kind of God-awareness.[2]

So we all have the inclination to recognize God, but most of us prefer to create a God-substitute, and this is true even of those who deny that they relate to God at all.

Through friends, experiences, insights, questions, losses, surprises, nature, and our search for meaning, God graciously gives us experiences of himself. Spirituality happens as life happens. It isn't restricted to hanging out in church or spending years in a cave. Spirituality grows out of life.

TWO TYPES OF SPIRITUALITY

Religion is very different from spirituality, falling into a different category entirely. It claims to have something astonishing: God on call and spirituality in the warehouse. Religion claims to have plenty of spirituality available for anyone who comes in and plays by the rules.

God, according to official church spokespersons, will shape your life if you'll just join up and join in.

I think that's a rather amazing claim, and I'm not surprised that a lot of people have trouble accepting it. I'm intensely interested in two approaches to spirituality. First, the version the church claims to regulate; and second, the spirituality of Jesus. Is the church's claim to dispense Jesus-brand spirituality a safe bet, a big con, or an offer that comes with a lot of small print that warrants a careful reading?

Consider the spirituality of one of America's major religions: the spirituality of sports. In the southern United States, there is a kind of Christian spirituality that is sanctioned by sports such as high-school football and basketball. Prayers are offered before games. Yes, teams representing public schools actually pray together. Many teams even have chaplains and hold devotions. Student organizations for Christian athletes meet in schools and churches. Athletes are known to give testimonies of their commitment to Christ and, hopefully, demonstrate that relationship by their actions on the field or court.

God is definitely on the team.

This spirituality places Christ and the experience of being a Christian in the context of sports culture. It's a culture in which the entire Christian life can be set in the context of competitive sports.

We have to ask: How similar is this spirituality to the spirituality of Jesus? And is it possible that it's tied much more closely to the American Christian idea of what it means to be a good high-school athlete? What does this kind of spirituality cause a person to value? What is the mission of this kind of Christian? What sort of community is created? How does this community read and apply the Scriptures? How does it lead to an authentic experience with God?

Because we can separate out the world of high-school sports from the regular world in which we live, we can see that sports-based spirituality can easily lead Christians to believe that God is overly concerned with the outcome of a game, the play-offs, the season, or injuries to key players.

And even if we believe that God is not confined to a particular set of influences, we recognize that our spiritual experiences are highly influenced by the things we associate most closely with God. For example, a young person may associate God with a particular style of music, a popular recording artist, a compelling public speaker, or a favorite church camp experience. For that person, God really "shows up" as they listen to Christian music or sit around a bonfire hearing campers share their personal testimonies.

This should start to sound familiar if you have noticed that Christian culture is busy "shaping" Christians with dozens of different agendas and methodologies. No one doubts the effectiveness of the church's methods to steep an individual Christian in a particular Christian subculture. But I doubt that they have much to do with Jesus.

What type of spirituality does a Christian develop from a multilevel marketing program that is closely aligned with a brand of Christianity? What might a Christian's spirituality look like if he or she grew up in a setting where faith was matched closely with an emphasis on weaponry and militarism? Or how might faith and spirituality develop in a setting where all participants are nearly identical ethnically, economically, socially, culturally, and politically?

And what would Jesus have to do with any of it?

CHURCH CONFORMITY OR EXPERIENCE OF GOD?

North American Christianity may have the distinction of having promised more of God and delivered less of God than any single act on the stage of church history. It's no wonder that books with promising titles such as *Experiencing God* sell millions of copies. Christians have been raised on hearing the constant announcement that knowing God is as simple as finding your seat in church on Sunday morning and then doing what the preacher says.

But when church members follow the instructions and don't experience God, they still experience spiritual hunger. They are hungry to know and experience the One whose presence was promised but then got overlooked.

We hear choruses of criticism and condemnation aimed at those who have left the church and those who, still within the walls, are critical and restless. We're constantly reassured that what the church and its activities deliver is the spirituality of Jesus. The evangelical movement is, if nothing else, supremely confident that Jesus is behind the church sign. He is in the sermons. He is at work in the music, the programs, and the kind of community the church presents to the world.

The real issue, we hear over and over, is people's willingness to come to church and relate to Jesus there. My own denomination promoted a campaign in which churches were urged to advertise themselves using a peppy slogan: First Baptist Church Is Connecting People to Jesus. If you think about it, that's quite a promise. In fact, it's a sobering one, particularly if we aren't just talking about explaining to people how to become a Christian but implying that a continuing relationship with Jesus comes through being present and involved in that church.[3]

I'm going to suggest that many, perhaps most, of those who are leaving the church or are about to leave are doing so because walking away seems to be the only path to authentic spirituality. In other words, if the leavers still hold out any hope of really connecting with Jesus, they know it will have to happen somewhere other than at church.

Before we start equating those who say they want spirituality and not religion with Oprah, Eckhart Tolle, and other preachers of the new age, we ought to look closely at what the leavers and critics are talking about. Before we conclude that those who walk away from churchianity are rejecting God, we might want to ask what were the chances they would genuinely find God within the communities that advertise Jesus Is Here?

I know a lot of church-leavers, and they aren't who you'd think. Many of them have left evangelical churches and found new homes in other Christian communions and traditions, often those that conservative Christians are convinced have "sold out" and gone "liberal."

I'm not minimizing the importance of theological and doctrinal clarity and biblical fidelity. It's a serious issue that I care about deeply. I am saying that a Jesus-shaped spirituality may not be dispensed within conservative evangelical churches as commonly and authentically as they advertise. The truth is that many of the leavers, and those about to leave, are headed in the direction of a Jesus-shaped Christianity when they walk out the church's door.

TRUE SPIRITUALITY VS. THE SYNTHETIC VARIETY

What kind of spirituality are many Christians finding on their plates when they go through the spiritual buffet line in the contemporary church? Evangelical Christians have church-growth spirituality, where the experience of knowing God is shaped by the activities of making the church bigger and its facilities more impressive. Thousands of pastors are practitioners of the spirituality that is measured by attendance figures, buildings, and budget; all part of a spirituality that Jesus repudiated. Yet millions of Christians are told this is the path to a genuine experience of God, as if God had agreed in advance to endorse whatever is done to make churches more successful.

We have a culture-war spirituality that produces Christians who might never share their faith but are ready at a moment's notice to debate politics, abortion, and civil unions for gay couples. It is a spirituality that calls down fire on its enemies and shapes its followers into intolerant soldiers waging a morality crusade. Its kingdom is the eventual triumph of moral conservatism, and its spirituality is conflict and argument.

Can we honestly say that Jesus was a culture warrior? Can we say that the spirituality of Jesus is geared to turning you into a noisy talk-radio pundit? Is our anger at the decline of culture really a dependable guide toward the experience of God?

We have a spirituality of emphasizing the Christian family as the central community in the Christian life. But what did Jesus say about the priority of the family? What did he say would often be necessary to be his follower? He said nothing to elevate the nuclear family; he actively redefined the family, and his actions bore out his words.[4]

We have a spirituality of worship experiences. We have a spirituality of prophecy and seeking revival. We have a spirituality that endorses the obsessive pursuit of doctrinal and theological precision. We have a spirituality of health, wealth, and prosperity.

Do any of these approaches to spirituality match Jesus-shaped spirituality? Is the transforming, revolutionary spirituality of Jesus residing in a quest for a bigger church building, a more moral society, a greater emphasis on traditional families, or a more detailed doctrinal statement?

I am convinced that people who say they are seeking spirituality and not the Christian religion are on the right path. If this offends you, let me ask: what is the other option? The only other option I can see is for Jesus-hungry people to try to content themselves with the religious junk food offered in the next new topical study, the bigger building program, the capital campaign, the latest attendance figures.

This option might make sense to you, and if it does, I understand why you are uncomfortable with too much talking about spirituality. But I can't support the organized religion option that is more concerned about statistics and size and image than it is about Jesus.

The problem does not lie with those who refuse to sit down, be quiet, open their wallets, and do what they are told. I don't believe for a moment that those who have abandoned organized Christianity have always found something better, but I'm sure they are looking for something better. I know, because I'm looking for the same thing.

I'm looking for a spiritual experience that looks like, feels like, sounds like, lives like, loves like, and acts like Jesus of Nazareth. It's that simple.

PART 2

THE JESUS BRIEFING

Recovering the Source
of a Christianity Jesus Would Recognize

6

Jesus or Vinegar

You probably already suspect this, but my primary purpose is to get you to think more intentionally about Jesus. Not an organization or a set of doctrines or even Christianity. But Jesus.

So far we've taken a close look at the painful and disappointing incongruities of the church, none of which is news to those of you who have already left the traditional church. And if you're still in the church, what I've said about the experience that many Jesus-followers have had with organized Christianity may have reopened old wounds.

In my own life, I try not to knuckle under to all the church pressures to conform. The church I attend and the denomination I am part of, both of which claim to represent Jesus, are not Jesus. Jesus never asked me to give to an organization the kind of exclusive devotion he demands from his disciples. Over and over, Jesus calls people to himself—out of the church, the culture, the economy, and the family.

He called a radical Jewish freedom fighter. He called a despised tax collector. He called at least three small businessmen. He called a hothead, a guy with easy ethics, some who struggled with oversize egos, and a few who had trouble accepting Gentiles. It's no different today. Jesus seems completely aware that in coming to him, we will leave other things behind, and that aspect of being involved with Jesus never stops. You don't leave your old life behind just once. You leave it behind every morning, every day.

Many who are leavers of religion are still followers of Jesus. These people already know something important about Jesus-shaped spirituality that many of us "stayers" have yet to figure out: when it comes to Jesus, read the labels carefully.

A few years ago my wife and I went to western Kentucky to visit my in-laws. Early one morning while it was still very dark, I woke up and was thirsty. I went to the kitchen and took a quick survey of what was available in the fridge. After deciding that orange juice and soy milk weren't what I wanted, I settled on a glass of apple juice. I took out the bottle, poured myself a glass, and drank up.

It was vinegar. You can fill in the dialog from there.

There are two aspects of this incident that should be noted. First, I made an assumption that the word "apple" on the label meant "delicious apple juice," and not "indescribably awful apple vinegar." Hey, seeing "apple" on the label was good enough for me. What else did I need to know?

Second, the shock of the experience was made worse by the fact that for at least thirty seconds, right up to the fatal moment of ingestion, I was expecting, imagining, pretasting in my mind delicious apple juice.

READ THE JESUS LABEL CAREFULLY

For many of us, the expected experience of God in Jesus has been replaced by the stunning vinegar of dysfunctional religion. Jesus is listed in big letters on the label, but there is little in the experience to indicate he's actually there. Perhaps your decision to leave the church behind is a way to wash the taste of religion out of your mouth. Your experience has made you wary of anyone who speaks about God, religion, the church, or Jesus. If that is you, I'd advise you to become a serious label reader.

As all label readers know, what's advertised in the big letters often bears little resemblance to what you are eating or drinking. Apple juice and apple vinegar have a lot of similarities but some very important differences. In the same way, I've learned that when Christians talk about

Jesus, or the God they believe came to earth in Jesus, I need to shift into full label-reading mode.

I teach Bible at a boarding school in eastern Kentucky. Every year I begin with a new crop of twenty-five to thirty young men and women who take the required introductory Bible course. One of the first assignments I give them is to go to a library and find ten contemporary cultural references to Jesus. What's to be learned in that assignment? In the Western world, we long ago passed the point where Jesus was someone only religious leaders could talk about. Jesus is now a corporate, political, and social symbol. He is appropriated by those who want to claim their products or agendas are recommended and endorsed by God. The image or mention of Jesus conveys authenticity in a way that nothing else can approach.

Notice where Jesus has been turning up.

Jesus is a vegetarian. Right up there on the billboard.

He's in favor of, and against, California's Proposition 8, which attempted to define marriage as between one man and one woman. Jesus often seems to be both for and against legislation that involves sexuality.

Jesus drives an environmentally sound hybrid car. He supports environmentalism, but he's also in favor of capitalism, coal, pollution, and global warming in instances where these things help people and on the days when he's not in favor of socialism, solar power, and pacifism.

Jesus is for the war and against it, for the American flag and against it, for militarized borders and against it. Jesus approves of all politicians, all political parties, and all political ideas, especially those that cost or save lots of money. He likes and hates big government. He's for and against all revolutions.

Jesus is a fan of all media and part of the panel of gods who approve of celebrities and whatever they are doing. He's frequently congratulated on Hollywood awards shows and has inspired every best album at the Grammys for decades.

Jesus will make you rich…or does he require you to be poor? Joel Osteen or St. Francis of Assisi? Or both?

Jesus loves America, only white people, only black people, all people, all children, just one church denomination (yours), and only those who are predestined for heaven.

Jesus wants the church on the corner to have a bigger building and is in favor of shutting down every bar in town. He loves prostitutes and sinners, but he polices the language people use. That's why the jury is still out on how he feels about preachers, prostitutes, and sinners who use too much profanity.

Jesus went to weddings and made the best wine in the Liquor Mart wine aisle. But he agrees with conservative evangelicals living in the American South that all drinking and most dancing are wrong. He's fine with square dancing and aerobics.

Jesus taught about hell but would never send anyone there. Jesus told a woman to go and sin no more, but he also redefined most everything, so it's not a sin anyway.

Jesus is understood only by the people to whom he speaks through the Holy Spirit, but he never says anything other than what's already clearly stated in the Bible. And on the very rare occasion when he does go beyond the written text, it's always in line with what a few high-powered academics tell us is there in the original Greek.

Jesus hates public schools and liberals, but he spent a lot of his short time on earth denouncing fundamentalists, religious leaders, and the wealthy, while befriending oppressed groups.

Jesus is what Christmas is all about, and he's against everything we do to celebrate it.

Jesus taught in a way that required explanation, but all kinds of people who haven't heard the explanations are 135 percent certain of what he meant in everything he said.

Jesus is the way, the truth, and the life and the only way to God, but he's decided that all religions are equal and no one can possibly be wrong. If you die, you're going to heaven courtesy of Jesus, who asks no questions.

Jesus started the church but has proven to be dicey about which church is the real one.

Jesus doesn't need your money but is happy to take it all and give you a tenfold return.

Jesus is a white American, a British actor, an oppressed black man, or the first gay man in the Bible.

Jesus was a Gnostic who made a home with his wife and kids. Or at least he was married in that one movie. So far.

Jesus is the property of historians, preachers, professors, and political theologians. But none of them really understand him, and a few aren't even sure he existed.

Jesus is actually Yeshua, Buddha, and Krishna, but these days he's going around in the body of a Puerto Rican preacher.

Jesus is God in the flesh, but that's really more of a metaphor than anything else.

We could add to the list, but the point has been made. If you've gotten the feeling that for most people Jesus is more symbol than substance, you aren't alone. It pays to carefully read any label that says Jesus.

PICKING JESUS OUT OF A CROWD

The label confusion doesn't stop at the church doors. While the options may be a bit less overwhelming inside the church, you'll still meet five (or more) favored characterizations of Jesus among his institutional followers. Consider these popular versions...

Jesus on the cross
This is where Jesus begins and ends for many Christians. Despite believing that Jesus arrived on earth as a newborn and came back to life after

being executed, the only thing Jesus did that makes any real difference for most people was that he died for the sins of the world. The tight focus on Jesus hanging on the cross is a version of Jesus where his other works, miracles, words, and overall mission are secondary. Sure he said some things and healed some people and taught people how to live. But all of that pales by comparison to preaching about the cross or focusing on the Eucharist.

Jesus the guru

This version sees Jesus' unjust execution on a Roman cross as the inevitable outcome of a good man living a life of love in a bad world, à la Martin Luther King Jr. What matters to these Christians is Jesus' teaching. If we could put the teaching of Jesus into practice, then we'd live like real Christians and the world would be a better, more peaceful place.

Jesus the miracle worker

This is the Jesus who solves problems by his superpowered ability to make bad things go away and good things happen. If he could cure a leper and bring corpses back to life two thousand years ago, he can deal with the problems people have today. Jesus the miracle worker is important in the present and has little real contact with the Jesus of the New Testament. He's mostly about hearing our prayers, changing things to match our desires, and sending miracles to whomever needs one.

Jesus the promoter

Jesus is always up to something big. He builds bigger churches, raises astounding amounts of cash, and sponsors huge religious events in stadiums. This version of Jesus can almost always be found in a venue with incredible music, entertaining video effects, and good-looking, upbeat speakers. He's the Jesus you meet when you find that awesome megachurch that has everything you need for a great religious experience.

Jesus the culture warrior

The culture-warrior Jesus is concerned about the public display of the Ten Commandments and the effect of Hollywood movies on your children. He fully approves of a number of political agendas, and his advice to his followers is to hunker down, take care of yourselves, and fight for America—a country that Jesus is particularly fond of. (No matter that he is a Palestinian Jew.)

WILL THE REAL JESUS PLEASE STEP FORWARD?

Of course, each of the church's versions of Jesus reflects something we know about him as he is presented in Scripture. Jesus did die on the cross and was raised from the dead for the sins of the world. These events are the centerpieces of the Christian Good News, but not the entire gospel message.

Jesus is a teacher whose message about the Kingdom of God is revolutionary and transformational, but incomplete by itself. I'm not faulting Jesus' importance as a teacher. His teachings deliver crucial knowledge. But Jesus is far more than just a motivational change agent. He gives people a new identity and a new life, not just better doctrine.

The Bible reminds us that God is a worker of miracles, and I would not neglect that aspect of his work. God is compassionate, merciful, and willing to rescue his people, but let's face it: Jesus doesn't always solve our problems. And our relationship with God, although it's based on grace, doesn't involve an ongoing series of God-directed events designed to smooth things out for us. God does not exist for our convenience. He is not a celestial vending machine that automatically dispenses a candy bar when we repeat the secret password or pray the right words. God is still God, and we're not.

Is Jesus involved in big religious projects? There is no question he is doing a big thing in history. His movement is advancing the biggest agenda ever: to bring all believing people from every nation into the Kingdom of God. God is a God of small things and large things, but he isn't always the God of what we define as a "big" thing. It's a mistake to equate Jesus with our ideas of importance or accomplishment, like attending a church that operates its own water park or having a laser show as part of the 11:00 a.m. worship service. It's wrong to assume that Jesus endorses your joining a church that's connected to your kids' school, which is connected to a Christian sports complex and a shopping mall, so you never have to mix with troublesome outsiders.

Is Jesus obsessed with public morality? He is the same God who gave us the Ten Commandments. He cares about what happens to children, families, and culture, but Jesus doesn't use morality to change the world, and he doesn't equip his followers with political weapons.

We could visit many other versions of Jesus currently on tour: the Health and Wealth Jesus, the Denominational Jesus, the Liberal/Fundamentalist Jesus, the Gender/Sexuality Jesus. In every case, there's a connection to the biblical Jesus that matters, as well as many ingredients that make apple juice taste like vinegar. So remember to read the label before you take a drink.

WHERE YOU'LL FIND THE "REAL" JESUS

Given the intellectual and spiritual climate of our culture and what I know about people who have left or are leaving the church, an obvious question would be, Why do we have to choose one version of Jesus over another? Shouldn't we seek out a both/and Jesus?

This touches on two bigger questions: Isn't it a mistake to claim to have cornered the market on the real Jesus? And isn't it arrogant to think that you, through study or research or prayer, have arrived at the most accurate, precise, truthful depiction of Jesus?

The claim of exclusivity and absolute authority, in any field, is offensive to contemporary people. Radio talk-show hosts know this and use it to their advantage, shouting their opinions as if the radio personality alone has a clear vision of "the truth." They are strident, argumentative, and irksome, knowing that their opponents won't be able to resist being baited. It generates a lot of publicity and attracts radio listeners. But is that a good strategy for Christians? And besides, aren't all ideas about Jesus somehow related to the "real" Jesus?

Jesus is like us and nothing like us

To understand Jesus and the God who comes to us in Jesus, we have to come to terms with the truth that Jesus is absolutely singular and unique. No matter how much research we might do, we can't define him. He is remarkably exclusive compared to the phony versions of Jesus running loose in our culture.

The first Christians lived in a world where there were not only hundreds of revered gods and deities but there also were people who demanded to be worshiped as gods. Practical polytheism and syncretism of religion was the order of the day. The easiest route for the Christian faith would have been to fit into this environment and say that Jesus was one of many gods or one of many deified men. Instead, the early Christians refused to compromise with their culture and insisted that Jesus was uniquely God, uniquely Lord of the universe, and a unique revelation of the God who made and ruled the universe. They died for this belief.

There is no confusion over what they believed. Jesus as God incarnate is not a novel idea that was cooked up years later, after Jesus' death and resurrection, by people who never knew him. Jesus was God before creation, he was God before he came to earth, he was God two thousand years ago while living on earth, he is God today, and he is God for eternity. Wherever true Christianity exists, it still has this character. While Jesus is like us in hundreds of ways, it is the ways that Jesus is uniquely, narrowly, exceptionally one of a kind that matter the most.

Living in between the ditches

I can tell you that if you become a Jesus-follower, and you seek to stay out of the twin ditches of cultural confusion about Jesus and church manipulation of Jesus, you will likely be shunned by the keepers of the religious institution. Now, as always, the genuine Jesus-follower walks a narrow path with a unique and exclusive Jesus. It is the road less traveled, and it does make all the difference. But why does this matter to someone who has left or is leaving the church and organized religion?

First, it matters that Jesus is one of a kind because there's good reason to recognize that the most popular versions of Jesus in religion and culture are deeply flawed and enormously deficient. Your experience of drinking apple vinegar instead of apple juice is a signal that the truth about Jesus can't be found just anywhere.

Second, it matters because Jesus is not offering you a watered-down, prostituted version of religion, morality, politics, and free entertainment. Completely on his own, without high-profile endorsements or appearances on *Entertainment Tonight,* he is compelling. And those who have followed him know his power and truth through changed lives and their willingness to give their lives for him. The counterfeits who are passed off as Jesus often are attractive, but in the way that a dime-store bracelet or deep-fried dough with powdered sugar is attractive. It might look good or taste good, but it's not real.

Jesus is compelling in the way the discovery of the stars or the experience of a one-of-a-kind romance is compelling. His presence draws you in to the deep.

Finally, coming to terms with the unique and exclusive Jesus matters because you have before you the possibility of a life-transforming adventure of coming to know Jesus for yourself, not through the various versions of Jesus others are selling. It is possible to meet him on his own terms, without any agenda. And it's deeply personal.

THE DAMAGING TESTIMONY OF VINEGAR PEOPLE

Several years ago I was having frequent conversations about Jesus with one of my students. She was drawn toward Jesus but wasn't yet convinced. One day she put her objection to me this way: "I don't want to become one of those people."

I knew what she was talking about. The Christians she knew didn't stand out because of their attachment to Jesus but by the unattractive baggage they carried. They had too much in common with the "vinegar" versions of Jesus: requirements about appropriate dress and what music you could listen to; expectations of regular church attendance and pledging allegiance to various forms of Christian culture; acceptance of rules, interpretations, and strictures that she couldn't connect with Jesus. I knew exactly what she meant.

You've probably seen the Mac versus PC commercials. These brilliant and simple ads have been magnificently successful for Apple because they reduce a product—and all the bad associations and assumptions about that product—to a single person. In the case of the PC, all its technology, design, and processing ability is reduced to a pudgy, overdressed, socially awkward, frustrated male who seems doomed to never have a good computer. "PC" is the embodiment of the unappealing, unreliable characteristics that Apple wants you to associate with a Windows-based personal computer.

Christians are the embodiment of what they believe. They are living, breathing products of a set of religious rules and beliefs, or they are transformed people who live in a daily relationship with Jesus. Sadly, many Christians come off like "PC." The problem isn't that we aren't cool. (It's pointless to be cool, because trying to make Jesus sexy is a waste of time.) The problem is in our legalism, materialism, judgmentalism, bigotry, arrogance, overconfidence, thoughtless words, bias toward outside institutions, prejudices, lack of love, and other vinegar versions of Jesus.

Jesus is completely unlike most of the stuff that Christians try to stick on him. Like it or not, the message about Jesus is distinctive, electric, and stunning, because there's nothing else like it. He is the Way, the Door, the One, and there is no one else who comes even close.

Every one of us is a spiritual being, whether we are atheists or the pope. There is within us a sense that the physical world and mortal life are incomplete, that there is a reality beyond us that isn't accessed by our five senses. We are drawn to something bigger, stronger, higher, better than what we know in everyday life. There is a tug and a hunger and a thirst for spiritual reality.[1]

That is what makes Jesus so appealing, even to nonreligious people. They long for living water and the bread of life. And too often, if they rely on Christians to give them a taste of these things, they get, instead of refreshment, a glass of vinegar. It may take years, or decades, to wash out the taste.

Start reading the Jesus labels more closely, because you can't get the good stuff just anywhere.

I want to invite you to reconsider Jesus. If you suspect you've been given an overly polite Jesus or an American Jesus or a spineless Jesus, you're probably right. If you are a typical church-leaver, you may be well on the way to following Jesus and discovering a new and transforming spirituality. Jesus, in his unapologetic narrowness and his claim to be like no one and nothing else, is the path to genuinely discovering God, love, hope, and direction for your life.

So let's see what we can learn about Jesus on his terms.

7

What We Can Know About Jesus

I was an incurable *X-Files* fan for most of its nine-season run in the 1990s. I've never been as devoted to a television drama as I was to the weekly adventures of FBI agents Fox Mulder and Dana Scully and their search for "the truth."

The X-Files was steeped in irony. There was always another layer to every story, a secret behind every small-town facade. The government was covering up the truth, and shadowy organizations were working to keep us in the dark about everything from a coming apocalypse to the presence of aliens on earth.

Yet in this murky and mysterious fog, Mulder and Scully worked relentlessly, at great risk to their lives, to uncover the true truth. Their devotion to the truth that was "out there" was unceasing.

Even as the show ended with much left unknown, the audience took away two messages: there was truth to be found, but there was no certainty anyone would ever finally know it.

The X-Files captured our culture's ambiguous approach to truth. We may talk about truth as if it is entirely personal, but we live as if it's "out there." Millions of people believe truth exists, but there's no promise it will ever be found. If you want to know the truth, be prepared to go against the grain of popular culture, and be prepared to hear the crowds, as well as the authority figures, telling you to stop wasting your time.

In this chapter and the next, I want to brief you on what I believe is the truth about Jesus. The truth is out there, but it will take *X-Files*-type curiosity and some courage to find it. The culture—including the academy—has decided to adopt the "any Jesus but the one in the New Testament" approach, while leaders of the church have asked Jesus to step into the wings and wait quietly while they keep the audience entertained. Either way, anyone looking for authentic, Jesus-shaped spirituality will have to undertake a Mulder-and-Scully operation.

You have probably tried before to search for truth that involves God. It's likely that you came up short, or were lied to, or felt you landed on truth but later were disappointed. If that's the case, it's worth another try. Because when you begin to discover the true truth about Jesus, you will know it's worth the effort.

Take, for example, best-selling author Anne Rice. A lapsed Catholic who married an atheist and abandoned the church, Rice became famous writing best-selling vampire novels. Then, several years ago, she began to pursue questions about Jesus. Today Anne Rice, after taking on the work of investigation, is a convincing advocate of a Jesus-shaped spirituality. She was rewarded with a new, life-changing experience of God through Jesus.

Some of what you'll read in this chapter and the next is known to almost everyone in our culture. For example, Christians believe and get the word out that Jesus is God. Jesus was executed even though he didn't commit a capital offense. Hundreds of people said they saw and talked to Jesus—alive again after he was buried. And Jesus is alive today.

Those are the widely reported parts of the Jesus story. But other important facts about Jesus have been denied, obscured, and deliberately tossed into the attic. What I'll share is a shorthand version of what scholars have come to believe after centuries of study. I can only scratch the surface and hope to inspire you to do more study on your own—or even better, to find teachers who can guide you.

Like Mulder and Scully trying to see beyond the government cover-up, I believe the truth about Jesus is out there, and that if we search for it, we can find it.

THE STARTING POINT

Before we move into the specifics about Jesus, I need to make it clear that no one, and certainly not me, knows all there is to know about Jesus. Neither is there complete agreement about everything that is known and everything that is true about Jesus. At the same time, it's a ridiculous misrepresentation to imply there's not a remarkable consensus among Christians on what we can know about Jesus.

Most of the important mistakes made about Jesus are big mistakes about major matters, not small ones. For example, there's no good reason to believe that Jesus was married, and few people believe it. It's an interesting what-if idea for a movie, perhaps, but it's not taken seriously by anyone you'd want teaching in a real classroom.

On the other hand, mistaking Jesus for a first-century version of Dr. Phil or Che Guevara rather than God in human flesh is a critical error with vast implications. There's a lot that can't be known about Jesus, but much of what was never recorded is inconsequential. Don't give up on knowing the essentials about Jesus just because you don't know the name of his second-grade teacher.

When a person follows Jesus, some beliefs are more necessary than others, and bringing them all together is important. For now, let's get the major components of a foundational knowledge of Jesus on the table.

Jesus is a Person, not an idea, a theory, a legend, a list, or a lecture. If you really want to get to know him, then read one of the four Gospels while living among people who are poor and suffering. Read the gospel of John in the waiting room of a children's cancer ward. Wash the feet of third-world citizens who live on the edge of a garbage dump. Talking about Jesus in theory, separate from the struggles and needs of real people, is usually an attempt to impress some religious bookkeeper but not a real pursuit of the Jesus who is worth following.

Jesus didn't dwell on ideas as much as he did the experience of real life. In other words, he taught his disciples primarily by asking them to follow him, and then they had three years to watch him in action. Don't mistake an essay that describes rock climbing with strapping on a helmet and climbing shoes, then going seventy feet up the face of a cliff.

When I was a kid, I took swimming lessons. There were no lectures in this class; every session was in the pool. Within a few weeks I was standing on a diving board looking at the deep end of the pool. My instructor was there, and so were my fellow students. I was terrified. Why was going in the deep end so necessary to learning how to swim?

Well, ask Jesus about that. It's exactly his method. You will learn the most about him when you are standing on life's diving board and he's telling you to jump into water that you've always avoided.

THE TRUE TRUTH ABOUT JESUS

Up to now, I have criticized organized Christianity and called it "churchianity." But Scripture teaches that the church serves an essential purpose when it conserves the truth about Jesus and passes on that truth to the rest of the world. And as much as the American church since the mid-twentieth century worked against a Jesus-shaped spirituality, I'm still not in complete despair. The church, on paper at least, continues to get out the true truth about Jesus.

If you're going to read the labels of what the church and the culture want you to believe, here's what you need to look for.

Jesus really existed

More and more, people are willing to give serious consideration to radical Jesus critics who suggest that Jesus was "constructed" from Jewish prophecies and the Messianic hopes of an ancient Middle Eastern tribe. Of course, there's always someone in the coffee shop who will say, "How do you know Jesus ever existed at all?"

Since Jesus didn't leave any archaeological proof of his existence, this may seem like a better objection than it actually is. In fact, none of the early enemies of Christianity—especially the Romans—questioned whether Jesus existed. They accepted as facts the broad outline of what we know about Jesus' bio and found it amazing anyone was worshiping someone who was executed by the state. I think they were in a good place to decide if Jesus was real or a myth.

If Jesus didn't exist, then his enemies would have trumpeted that fact. But instead, they offered insulting commentary on his life, never questioning his death on the cross. Neither did they dispute the fact that a movement existed long after Jesus died nor that the adherents worshiped him as God.

We're talking about a Person who showed up in history. The lack of a YouTube video doesn't lessen the certainty that Jesus did exist and did change the world profoundly.

Jesus was Jewish

On the fringes of those who study Jesus are a few who want to make Jesus more Asian, Greek, or Roman. Avoid them. Everything solid we know about Jesus puts him firmly in a first-century, eastern Mediterranean, lower-middle-class Jewish world. This is important for many reasons, from Jesus' physical appearance to our attitude toward followers of Jesus living in the Middle East today. Despite the many media depictions of Jesus in film as British or American, we have to keep in mind that he was a thoroughly Middle Eastern man who lived completely in that culture.

Of course, first-century Jewish culture in Galilee was a lot less Jewish and a lot more cosmopolitan than most people realize. Jesus grew up only a few miles from a major city with a theater and plenty of Greco-Roman culture. He would have spoken a bit of at least four languages just to do business in his community. He surely saw a great deal of political violence during his life, knew people we would call terrorists, and understood the impact of other cultures on his own.

In the Gospels, Jesus routinely speaks to issues that are easily misunderstood without a basic appreciation of his Jewish context. For instance, consider the story of Jesus talking with the woman at the well.[1] It's important to know it caused a scandal because she was female and not related to Jesus and she was a Samaritan. She was a member of a racially and culturally despised class in Jesus' time. Jews and Samaritans disliked one another on a level that far exceeds the antagonism between Yankees and Red Sox fans.

I don't believe, however, the Jewishness of Jesus means we should give extreme emphasis to how a knowledge of Judaism leads us to a radically Jewish Jesus and a deeply Judaized Christianity. When I hear a teacher start referencing little-known rabbinic practices and claiming they are the actual fine print of the four Gospels, I wince and hit the Off button. The overriding message of Jesus' earliest followers was that Christian faith was not primarily for Jews. It was for everyone.

History shows that the story of Jesus' life, death, and resurrection quickly came to dominate the non-Jewish world. Among the most serious questions the early Christians answered had to do with how much of Jewish religion and culture could be accepted in the Christian movement. The answer was overwhelmingly consistent: Jesus and his message came from a Jewish birthplace, but they were for the entire world and shouldn't be confined to the Jews.

Jesus fulfilled all that his religion ever taught, and he transcended every cultural norm. He is, after all, the Savior of all humanity, not just the Jews.

Jesus didn't operate within a democratic system

One aspect of Jesus' world that is essential to understand is that his life and teachings, and the movement he started, all took place in occupied territory. Galilee and Palestine, as the Romans first called it, were under the oppressive domination of the Roman Empire. Jesus was a member of an oppressed race that traced its captivity back to the Babylonian deportation five hundred years earlier. And long before that, the Hebrews spent four hundred years as slaves in Egypt. Nothing occupied the people of Jesus' world like the idea of wanting to finally be set free from oppression. They looked forward to the time when God would establish his Kingdom on earth, with God's King paying back and tossing out all their enemies.

This means that much of what Jesus said and did was first interpreted in a controversial and quite explosive political context. It was, after all, the Romans who executed Jesus for claiming to be the King of the Jews, a title the occupiers had rented out to the Herod family. Jesus entered Jerusalem for the last time in the traditional way of Israel's kings: riding on a donkey, hailed as the long-awaited Son of David, and in the shadow of a Roman barracks. He proclaimed the Kingdom of God as if he were the King that all Jews had been waiting for. He spoke about the authority of God and not about the authority of Caesar. He told Pilate that the ruler's power was on loan from God.

This rhetoric and Jesus' actions were dangerous. The Romans weren't much for writing your name on the chalkboard and assigning after-school detention. They crushed all potential rebels hard and fast.

It may help us to remember that as I write these words, the United States military is occupying the nation of Iraq. We know much about the emotions and responses that this has stirred among the Iraqi people. It is in a similar context, a nation that was occupied and controlled by a foreign power, that Jesus carried out his mission. If we miss what this contributes to what we know about Jesus, we'll certainly misunderstand him.

Perhaps one of the most radical things Jesus said was that his Kingdom was not of this world, but that he would one day return to earth when God establishes his Kingdom. In the context of the Roman Empire, this was explosive talk with explosive implications about Jesus. The conclusion that Jesus is Lord and God is not a religious affirmation. It's a message that threatened to pull down the world's most powerful empire.

Jesus accepted the Hebrew Scriptures, with conditions

One of the problem areas for many people is a tendency to disconnect Jesus from the Bible that he knew very well. That Bible of the first century was the Hebrew Bible, almost identical to today's Protestant Old Testament, and made up of law, prophets, and miscellaneous writings, all of which Jesus refers to.

The problem is that the Old Testament is full of matters that are hard to interpret and understand. For example, do Jesus' words about nonresistance to enemies contradict the many instances when God ordered Israel to annihilate an enemy in war? Or what would Jesus say about the Old Testament condemnation of men lying with men in Leviticus 18? For many people, the easy route has been to place Jesus in the position of either rejecting the Old Testament or presenting entirely new ideas and messages that depart from Old Testament teaching.

It's not that clear-cut. Reading the New Testament, we see that Jesus believed, taught from, and honored the Old Testament with the highest confidence. While we don't know how Jesus would have read or understood everything in the Old Testament, his use of books such as Leviticus, Daniel, Isaiah, Deuteronomy, Genesis, and Psalms makes it clear that he placed these scriptures in a place of authority.

But didn't Jesus openly disagree with a number of Old Testament teachings? Many times he stated: "You have heard it said, but I say to you..." Don't be too quick to mark that down as rejection. In actuality, Jesus was going to the core, the deepest meaning, of Old Testament commandments such as "don't commit adultery." He shifted the emphasis from outward behavior to the condition of a person's heart, the inner person.

Even more important than how Jesus read Scripture is how Jesus saw himself in relation to Scripture. He emphasized, in a stunning demonstration of either ego or truth, that the Bible was about him. While it may be frustrating to not have a good answer for what Jesus thought about every story and statement in the Hebrew Scriptures, it is an incredible help to know that Jesus considered his life to be the center point and deepest meaning of the Bible.

Clearly, the New Testament writers were excited by this idea. Books such as Hebrews and John's gospel constantly point out that the entire Old Testament project found its end point in Jesus' life, death, resurrection, and reign. This is one reason why the New Testament moves away from "religion" as God's way of dealing with the world and offers Jesus as the one Mediator between God and humans.

Since all the Bible is "keyed" to the tune of Jesus, it directs our entire approach to the Bible. For those people who have felt bashed and bullied by the way Christians use the Bible to control behavior (don't drink or have any fun) and prove that God favors one particular political party (arguing that President Barack Obama is either a Muslim or the Antichrist), this is a huge, positive development.

Jesus is the incarnation of the One God

On a list of beliefs about Jesus, this one sounds pretty heavy, and it is. It's the single biggest idea Christianity has to offer. If you don't see it on the label, my advice is to beware of whatever you have in your hand.

The core claim of Christianity is that God entered the human race as one of us—a Guy named Jesus from the backwater village of Nazareth. It took four centuries for the Christian movement to stop feuding and just say that Jesus is both God and human, fully and equally. No amount of descriptive language, metaphors, illustrations, explanations, or theological book-throwing can move us beyond the mind-boggling assertion that God chose to become fully human, as the Nicene Creed says, "for us and for our salvation."[2]

In the first century, when Jesus was first worshiped, people commonly believed in deified human beings and gods in the form of humans. Everything from a pop-up toaster to the town hooker had a patron god. Adding Jesus to this pantheon would have been simple and safe, but the early Christians insisted that Jesus was not another god, but the *one and only* God. Christians called Jesus "the image of the invisible God," "the fullness of God in a human body," "the Word became flesh," and the "only Son" of God.[3]

Considering that the one fact most people knew about Jesus was that he was executed as a loathsome criminal, such claims seemed beyond ridiculous.

It is all the more amazing that the early Christians would believe Jesus was God when we realize that the first generation of believers was Jewish, and Judaism has this Ten Commandments thing that prohibited anything approaching the worship of a human being. Judaism also was the first monotheistic faith, which meant a faithful Jew would have great difficulty picturing the Lord as a local carpenter.

The early Christians prayed to Jesus, worshiped him, and taught and preached that he rightly possessed equality with God. This wasn't just an interesting idea to ponder; it was blasphemy in the eyes of the Jewish authorities. But regardless of how many religious absolutes and longstanding traditions it violated, the belief that God became human in Jesus is crucial. Without the incarnation, whatever we call "Christian belief" collapses. The incarnation was a no-compromise foundational issue, and it remains so today. The incarnation may be the greatest stumbling block that Christianity places in the road of spirituality, but that stumbling block is the cornerstone of everything Christians believe about Jesus.

The incarnation has many wonderful aspects, but my favorite is this: the incarnation is the complete refutation of every human system and institution that claims to control, possess, and distribute God. Whatever any church or religious leader may claim in regard to their particular access to God or control over your experience of God, the incarnation is the last word: God loves the world. God came into the world in the form of the people he created, the human race (including you and me), who bear his image. God's creation of humanity in his image gives hints of who he is, since we all are marked by his fingerprints.[4]

But as flawed humans, we give only a vague hint of God. Our broken reflection of God's image is easily drowned out by our broken humanity. Then, two thousand years ago, God came in his fullness. He came to all of us in Jesus. The incarnation is not owned, trademarked, or controlled by any church. It belongs to every human being. The incarnation is not something that requires a distributor or middleman. It is a gracious gift to every person everywhere, religious or not. God gave himself to us in Jesus.

For Christians, Christmas is the season when we think the most about the incarnation. It is the story of God becoming a baby, born in a stable to a young girl no different from millions of other human mothers. Except for one thing: the girl was a virgin and bore the Son of God. It is easy for me to get misty when I see manger scenes or hear the great carols declaring in some of the oldest Christian language that this Child is "God of God, Light of Light."

A few years ago I visited a church where the minister had lost his faith in the incarnation. I don't know why he had rejected the central affirmation of Christian faith, but on this Christmas Eve as we visited his church, he tried to attach important meaning to the Christmas season without proclaiming that God took on human flesh in the birth of Jesus.

If I were in his shoes, I would speak about anything but Jesus, but this skeptical minister tried to tell the Christmas story as a morality tale, hoping to illicit our pity for the poor and the homeless. There were Mary, Joseph, and the baby, the shepherds and the angels...all the cast of a good Christmas story. Only one character was missing. Not the friendly beasts or the little drummer boy. Not the innkeeper or the wise men.

No, God was missing. God, coming to this world as an infant. God in a smelly stable. God under his starry sky. God worshiped by shepherds. God coming to a world in the dead of night, bringing a light we could never bring ourselves.

Without God, listening to that Christmas sermon was a vinegar experience. You see, without the incarnation, Christianity isn't even a very good story, and most sadly, it means nothing. "Be nice to one another" is not a message that can give my life meaning, assure me of love beyond brokenness, and break open the dark doors of death with the key of hope.

The incarnation is an essential part of Jesus-shaped spirituality. Which brings us to the second part of our attempt to read the Jesus labels more clearly. Let's continue.

8

Accepting the Real Jesus

I grew up attending a large, revivalistic, fundamentalist Baptist church in western Kentucky. By the time I was baptized at age fifteen, I must have heard the phrase "accept Jesus" at least five thousand times. It may have been ten times that many.

In Sunday school I heard a few stories about Jesus. I knew about the crucifixion and resurrection. I heard phrases like "Jesus is the Son of God" and "Jesus should be the Lord of your life." I really had no idea what such things meant.

The year after I was baptized, I took a church-sponsored class on Baptist doctrine. (I still have the book.) It took the language of our congregation's confession of faith and explained it. I was hungry to learn.

Jesus got one chapter and brief parts of a few others. I completed the class still largely clueless about Jesus. I trusted my church to tell me what the Bible said and how I was supposed to live. And in my fervor as a new Christian, I was eager to share my faith.

But the out-of-balance view of Jesus continued until my senior year of college, when I needed to take an elective in my religion major. I went to my New Testament professor and asked to do an independent-study project. He balked but then sized me up and assigned a fifty-page paper on "The Idea of the Good in the Teachings of Jesus." I asked for it, and I got it: a lot of time with Jesus.

For the next three months, I did something I'd never done before: I lived in the four Gospels. Not picking out a verse here and there to support my church-shaped spirituality, but actually reading the Gospels on their own terms. I was digging into the life and teachings of Jesus to answer my thesis question.

It won't surprise you to learn that spending three months with Jesus shook my safe Baptist assumptions to the core. The world inside the Gospels was not the same as the world in my church. Jesus didn't talk like a Baptist. The issues that my church obsessed over (drinking, separation from the world, movies and television, denominational superiority) weren't on the radar.

Spending three months with Jesus did something else. I was a young preacher, but for the first time in my life, I realized I didn't understand the Jesus I was proclaiming. I was religious from head to toe. But Jesus? In the Gospels, I discovered that Jesus was another world, another universe. I knew him as the actor in the story as it was told to me by my church. I hadn't discovered how much more there was to the story.

When you pursue Jesus-shaped spirituality, you do it on Jesus' terms. And Jesus wastes no time letting you know he's not a Protestant or an American. The more time I spent with him, the clearer it became that he didn't seem to have a strong opinion on card playing, movie watching, dancing, or the other demonized "worldly" influences. I'm still somewhat in shock to know that the wine Jesus made in John 2 wasn't Welch's grape juice. At age twenty-one, I had to admit that my church-shaped faith wasn't always a dependable guide to Jesus.

JESUS ON THE JESUS-SHAPED LIFE

If we are hungry for a Jesus-shaped life, what is it about Jesus that will most shape our lives to be like him? To answer that question, we'll have to cut our ties to the comfort and safety of traditions, customs, and assumptions. It's time to leave behind our religious biases that have no connection to Jesus and begin a real adventure.

Jesus preached, taught, and demonstrated the presence and priority of the Kingdom of God.

The four Gospels are full of the language of God's Kingdom. Jesus' teachings, parables, miracles, sermons, and sayings repeatedly emphasize the Kingdom of God (or "Kingdom of Heaven" in Matthew's gospel.) A simple statement from the gospel of Mark summarizes Jesus' preaching: "The kingdom of God is at hand; repent and believe in the gospel."[1] Even on the eve of his execution, Jesus was telling Pilate what God's Kingdom was all about.

What comes to mind when you think of the Kingdom of God? I can tell you what I was taught. Preachers and Bible teachers in my church tradition forced every one of Jesus' Kingdom references into one of two niches: either they addressed heaven or they referred to a future reign of Christ on earth. They never had anything to do with our life in the present.

In other denominations, people were being told that their church was the Kingdom of God. In other words, if you were part of that church, you were in the Kingdom.

I was in my twenties before I finally realized that Jesus' dozens of references to the Kingdom of God were almost all about something happening at the very moment he was speaking. Only a small minority of his references to the Kingdom referred to a future, fully arrived Kingdom.

In real time, in around AD 29, God was revealing the Kingdom. The Kingdom of God didn't look like other kingdoms. The King of the universe was here, planting and inaugurating his Kingdom. But his reign was well disguised as the ragtag movement of a Jewish carpenter who saw the world in upside-down terms.

Every one of Jesus' miracles was a demonstration of the Kingdom. His acts of compassion and inclusion were demonstrations of the Good News of the Kingdom. He was teaching his followers to see the Kingdom, plant the Kingdom, and be the Kingdom.

Until the Kingdom of God arrives in its final form, to be a follower of Jesus is to be tuned to the presence and power of the Kingdom of God in the present. Whatever we do as individual Jesus-followers or as communities living for Jesus, we do it as part of the Kingdom of God in the world.

The Kingdom perspective will separate the merely religious from those who eagerly seek a Jesus-shaped life. You can't be a subject in Jesus' Kingdom—especially as he describes it—and have your own little fiefdom and alternate Kingdom. Jesus-shaped spirituality can't be confined to one church, one tradition, or one set of unquestioned rules. The Kingdom of God isn't under any person's control. We discover the Kingdom as we follow Jesus.

Jesus practiced radical inclusion of those who were excluded.

I can't fully describe how annoyed I get when someone starts in on the lamebrained discussion of "does God love everyone?" The unspoken assumption behind the question is that surely God loves Christians more than anyone else.

What should a Jesus-follower's attitude be toward adherents of other religions or of no religion? In church circles, the questions sound like these: Do we have to let those rowdy kids play basketball on church property? What should we do if homeless people ask to sleep in our building? What will we do if a gay couple shows up to attend a worship service here? And, of course, Why do we waste so much money on the hunger fund?

In the 1960s, the American South was filled with Bible-preaching churches that hadn't gotten around to admitting that God sent Jesus to save all kinds of people. According to the book of Ephesians, Jesus destroys the walls of separation between races, genders, preferences, and labels. The book of Revelation shows God's ultimate goal: a multicultural Kingdom where every kind of person is offering worship to the King out of their own uniqueness.

Jesus lived in a world that enforced a strict holiness code. It was not just a social custom; it was a serious political and religious expectation. If you violated the rules of who was "good/bad" or "clean/unclean," you were placing yourself in the gun sights of the theological police. To the most serious of Jewish patriots, being too generous toward outsiders amounted to sedition.

Of course, Jesus was a Man on a mission when it came to deconstructing the "who's in/who's out" code. He had his own idea of who was acceptable. He touched lepers, talked to women, allowed women to talk to him, allowed a sick "unclean" woman to touch him, heard the prayers of non-Jews, befriended Samaritans and sexually immoral people, forgave adulteresses, dined with tax collectors, befriended prostitutes, and went to parties with sinners. I'm still checking to find what he did with lawyers, but I'm sure they'd be included as well.

Jesus chose not to follow the same rule book as the Jewish religious authorities. Neither did he abide by the Baptist behavior code that I grew up with. He didn't teach that we fortify our righteousness by keeping rules and avoiding contact with sinners. He taught that we have all sinned, that God loves us all, and that we all are included in the Kingdom God is building. If God doesn't avoid us, as flawed and desperate as we are, then the debate over how we relate to other people is over. We relate to all people, no matter how different they might be from the Christian norm.

If you adopt the practice of the Jesus-shaped life, you will run into Christians who are deeply troubled by what you're doing. Jesus was condemned by religious leaders. His own family, and some of his closest disciples, objected to his choice of friends. Jesus wasn't surprised by any of this. In one of his best-known parables, the older brother in the story of the prodigal wasn't about to attend a party that honored his wayward brother. I'm sure Jesus met plenty of real-world older brothers who were just as sanctimonious and just as right, and were completely wrong.

If you are going to experience the Good News that God has come into the world to save you, that he is inviting you to know him in and through Jesus, you'll have to deal with your boundaries, walls, and prejudices.

Are you avoiding your gay sister? Can't forgive your son for being arrested? Are you standing aloof from the poor, the immigrants, or family members who have hurt you? Do you have no love for Muslims, those who support abortion rights, advocates of big government, or fundamentalists? Jesus is going to take you to those people, and he's going to gently, persistently show you that his heart embraces the ones you refuse to embrace. He forgives those who have hurt you, so that you will have that moment when the acceptance of God changes the kind of person you are and how you view people.

Jesus was constantly engaged in producing disciples.

As we look at Jesus and his life, we can't avoid observing the lives of those who were closest to him. Much of the work Jesus did in his three years of active ministry was to train twelve men. It's clear from reading the Gospels that discipleship is the most basic identity of a Christian. But it's also easy for this truth to be obscured by debates and theological hairsplitting.

If you've left the church, it might be because you got tired of the tiresome debates about who is in and who is out. Who are the people God accepts, and which ones does he reject? These are questions that fascinate seminary professors, a lot of pastors, and nearly all evangelists. Does God do business only with those who have said the right prayer, or those who signed on to the accepted faith statement, or those who have been vetted by the elder board?

Side issues tend to occupy center stage, while the real question is this: What is a Christian and what is it, exactly, that a Christian is supposed to be? It's a question that deserves an answer, and there is a simple, outwardly visible indicator. It's reliable, and it's straight from the Bible.

The word *Christian* is used twice in the Bible. It is far from the most common term that was used to identify the followers of Jesus. And perhaps in modern church culture, the word has been at the center of so many disagreements that we need to adopt a more accurate, more biblical term. *Believers? Jesus-followers?* No matter what we call ourselves, it's important to answer the question of what we are supposed to be, and it's not difficult to find a clear biblical answer.

Jesus-shaped spirituality is best described as discipleship. Jesus told the twelve apostles to make disciples, which Jesus defined as "baptizing them…[and] teaching them [his followers] to observe all that I have commanded you."[2]

There may be people who believe in Jesus who are not disciples, but that is not what he was seeking to produce. Jesus' assignment to the apostles was not to get people to respond to an altar call but to make disciples of all nations. And he defined that as being taught to obey everything he commanded. Obedience is action, not merely a set of beliefs.

We need to find the answers to three critical questions related to discipleship: First, what is a disciple's relationship to Jesus? Second, what are the processes that produce a disciple? Third, how does a disciple live? Jesus isn't looking for admirers; he's enlisting followers. The reason the church got distracted from Jesus-shaped Christianity was that discipleship got lost in the fog of church traditions, human rules, and religious culture.

The Gospels' portraits of individual Christians present us with a great variety of people. There is tremendous diversity among them in terms of temperament, age, marital status, station in life, even race and religious background. But what is true of all of them is that they were disciples. They followed Jesus in obedience to his teachings, commands, and example.

One other thing we can't escape is that the spiritual journeys of the saints we meet in Scripture, both Old Testament and New, are highly individualized. Abraham was waiting for his father to pass away. Jacob was being a pain. Moses was dealing with his confused sense of identity. Peter was working for a living. Paul was a religious fanatic. It should give anyone hope to know there's really no place in your life journey where God will not condescend to begin working in your life, if you are willing.

As diverse as the spiritual journeys are, however, they all have the same destination. God does not want to produce believers, religious people, or a particular kind of culture. God's goal in Scripture is to produce people whose life journeys have four unmistakable compass points:

- Knowing God as Father through his Son, Jesus.
- Experiencing forgiveness and a right relationship with God through Jesus.
- Becoming a follower of Jesus in community with other disciples.
- Participating in the mission and life of the Kingdom of God in the world.

This is what it means to be a Christian. It is the life of a disciple, which is lived in four dimensions: knowing God; a cross- and Christ-centered faith; following Jesus as a community project; and being a citizen and servant in the work of God's Kingdom. In the pursuit of Jesus-shaped spirituality, this approach to discipleship is a line in the sand. Discipleship produces a person with a growing awareness of God as he came to us in Jesus. Distorted ideas of God are poison to the soul, no matter how admirable their source. The invitation to know God as our Father is his greatest gift to us.

It has been amazing to hear some of the criticism of William Young's book *The Shack*. While it's far from a perfect book, it is a book that speaks deeply to the desire in the heart of every Christian to know "Papa," a God who is our Friend, who loves us and is for us. The noisy opposition to the book on the grounds that it fails to portray the God of the Bible shows that many Christians still have not grasped one of the Bible's most basic truths: God is a loving, tender, attentive, gracious Father.

Jesus-shaped spirituality is cross centered and Christ centered. The

Good News of the Kingdom of God is the Good News that the King died to save us.

We will never be perfect disciples. We will constantly fail in ways large and small. None of us will live a day that we do not need the mercy and grace that were poured out through Jesus on the cross. A Kingdom-seeking disciple lives in the light of the cross and in the grace of the perfect Mediator and dies confessing that Jesus has defeated death.

Jesus-shaped spirituality hears Jesus say "believe and repent," but the call that resonates most closely in the heart of a disciple is "follow me." The command to follow requires that we take a daily journey in the company of other students. It demands that we be lifelong learners and that we commit to constant growth in spiritual maturity. Discipleship is a call to me, but it is a journey of "we."

For millions of Christians, the great failure of the church is its failure to be a resource for producing and encouraging the life of discipleship. Instead of discipleship, the church has taught a life of rule keeping, with the rules set not by Jesus but by religion and traditions. Long ago the church replaced the Kingdom of God with church activities and priorities.

Finally, the Jesus-shaped disciple is a citizen of the Kingdom and a servant in the Kingdom. As we will see in a moment, Jesus is a movement starter. He is not warehousing Christians or starting a museum of righteousness. There is a world for us to go into and hundreds of ways to serve Christ in that world by serving others. One of Jesus' great passions was teaching his disciples to see the Kingdom in the faces of marginalized people—the last, least, lost, and little.

There is little need for large churches stuffed with satisfied audiences. There is a great need for a movement of disciples going into the overlooked places of the world to see and serve the Kingdom of God.

Jesus is the only Mediator between God and humanity.

If a person were going to make a thoroughly bad characterization of Christianity, I can think of two ways to do it. One would be to catalog all the nonsense that has reduced Christianity to a message for individuals to get saved and forgiven by believing Jesus died for them on the cross. The other mischaracterization would be to overlook the fact that a great deal of the gospel is about individuals being saved by Jesus, who died for their sins on the cross.

Those who despise Christianity find its teaching that "Jesus saves" to be quaint and hokey. But the deepest practitioners of Christianity, even when they have lost everything else, hold on to the fact that Jesus died and rose again, and he did it for them. Jesus does save.

Crucial to a life of Jesus-shaped spirituality is the place of Jesus as the one sufficient Mediator between God and humanity, in contrast to relying on religious institutions and rituals that insist on occupying the stage with Jesus. The radical nature of believing "Jesus = salvation" and "Salvation = Jesus + nothing" becomes clearer as we have to move through a culture where the church has attempted to replace Jesus as our connection to God.

It is not the place of a church to claim that Jesus has outsourced any portion of the responsibility for our standing or relationship with God. Whatever we mean by church membership (which I am in favor of, generally) or whatever the relative importance of church ministries, there is not a single place where the church can do more than simply point to Jesus as the complete Source of salvation. Once the church begins speaking of itself as "necessary," it has overstepped.

The only necessary things are what Jesus gives freely and graciously. The only basis for salvation is Jesus and his perfect life, death, and resurrection. He is the one assurance.

Jesus' movement proclaims the gospel, encourages disciples, and witnesses to the presence of the Kingdom.

Jesus launched a world-changing movement with twelve men. It is a cross-cultural church-planting movement that is committed to spreading the gospel, making disciples, and extending God's Kingdom. That much is clear from reading the Bible.

I realize that it might come as a surprise to you that in looking at the life of discipleship, I am emphasizing that the church is part of following Jesus. (Up to now, I have not gone easy on organized Christianity.) Jesus started a movement that was to continue after he was physically gone from the earth, a movement that would continue his mission, produce disciples, and proclaim Jesus as Lord.

If Jesus did not intend to start a movement, then much of what he did, particularly in the training and teaching of the apostles, was pointless. The closing chapters of three of the four Gospels, and the opening chapters of the book of Acts, make it clear that Jesus planned for the movement he began in Galilee to continue "to the ends of the earth."

The issue for many of us is how does Jesus' movement relate to the church as we've experienced it, particularly in the Christian West? My answer is simple: not dependably and often not well. I have serious doubts that Jesus would recognize the multimillion-dollar salaries, programs, and facilities or the ongoing competition for church attendance as being anything close to what he began. If you look hard enough, you can find descriptions of the early church that share points of contact with today's churches. A few examples include Christians who gather for worship, hear teaching, have leaders, and observe the sacraments, or church ordinances of baptism and the Lord's Supper. These points of contact, however, don't rescue much of the Western church from the dilemma that it doesn't look like Jesus, act like Jesus, or promote the agenda of Jesus.

Tens of millions of Christians in China are part of a mighty movement that looks and acts like Jesus. It is a church largely without property. It is a church with intense love and a willingness to suffer. It is a church that is deeply impacting a culture from the inside through influence and faithfulness. It is producing millions of disciples.

The Chinese church movement has no megachurch facilities, no seminaries, no Christian music industry, no retreat centers, no youth-ministry specialists, no recreation centers, no highly paid pastors, and no high-powered technology. While this church movement isn't perfect, it is a powerful reminder that the church as Jesus conceived it can and does exist. That same church can exist all over the world. Practitioners of a Jesus-shaped spirituality must learn to discern it.

We've come to the end of our Jesus briefing. I could have said much more about Jesus, but these essential truths will help us "read the labels" of spirituality and religion. With this foundation, we can avoid the vinegar of an alternative Jesus promoted by a wayward church or a confused culture. We now know what we are looking for, and we have some idea of how it all comes together in Jesus.

Now it's time to look at what the New Testament does with the Person we've examined. We want to look deeply at what we mean by "living a Jesus-shaped discipleship." What is the Christian life, and what could possibly make it reasonable to try to live as a Christian today?

9

What Jesus Is Doing in the World

After writing the two previous chapters, briefing you on some of the essential truths about Jesus, I'm anticipating some suspicion on your part. You could be thinking: *You're trying to drag me back inside the church, aren't you?*

Good question. I think it's time we all got our cards on the table, starting with me.

If I were to write a book defending the church from all detractors, seasoning it with a generous amount of finger-pointing and blaming of people who dare criticize or abandon the church, I'd sell a lot of books to the usual gallery of nodding Christians. I'd be reviewed positively on all the right Christian blogs. I'd get hugs, and I like hugs.

There have been times that I would have written that book. For seventeen years I collected my paycheck from churches, and I did all I could to get people in the door. I said whatever was necessary. I preached sermons in defense of the church, and I did things I don't want to think about to show that the church had first place in my priorities.

Having been in church all my life, I met plenty of people who knew how to stick a Jesus smiley face on the front of whatever the church was doing. I knew all the right biblical language about Jesus, and I used that language to wallpaper the sanctuary of whatever church I belonged to.

If you had known me then and had told me that you'd left the church, I would have responded with the following:

1. You're a sinner who is avoiding God.

2. You need to read the Bible and get your thinking straight.
3. Whatever your experience of the church happened to be, it doesn't get you off the hook. You're supposed to be there. God demands it!

The finger-pointing church felt good to me. I was comfortable there. And I have no idea when it all started to come unglued. But my experiences as a paid staff member were, to say the least, a constant challenge to the idea that churchianity and Christianity were the same thing. All along I had been willing to accept the church and its priorities as being the very things that Jesus endorsed. If the prevailing assumption was that Jesus would happily get on board with whatever the church decided to do (and that was, in fact, the assumption), well, it was all right with me.

THE NEXT STEP AFTER FINGER-POINTING

And then it fell apart for me. I didn't abandon the church, but I did go through a number of phases that may sound familiar to you. I investigated at least nine alternatives, hoping to find a different form of church that rang true with what I knew of Jesus. They were these, listed in random order:

Church renewal

This was the terminology we used in the seventies to say something was terribly wrong and we needed to make it right by tinkering with ministerial titles and inventing a few new programs. But tinkering didn't get the job done.

Church revival

In this phase we begged God to straighten out the church and society through a huge movement of the Holy Spirit. Some denominations actually have committees on revival, where they vote on when and how God should move. I'm not kidding.

Small groups

This was a movement in which churchgoers could get together with a small number of people and try to think as little as possible about the mess we were experiencing in the larger church. We hoped we'd be able to develop quality relationships and invest less in pretending to be spiritual. But mostly we griped.

The charismatic movement

Once again we hoped that the Holy Spirit was supernaturally breathing life into a sold-out church as the end of the world approached. For me, this turned into the hyperspiritual Church Olympics, and I kept coming in last. I never could muster as much outward spiritual passion or as many manifestations as the people around me.

The true church

This was the ongoing search conducted by Christians who were convinced, that out there somewhere, there had to be a denomination that got everything right doctrinally and practiced the actual stuff that was in the Bible. In advanced cases this can manifest itself by consecutively trying out several major denominations but always discovering there is one more that you haven't yet checked out. And it's just possible that *that* is the one that comes a little closer to being the true church.

The Catholic and Orthodox churches

Perhaps those guys were right after all? They have maintained their rites and rituals for sixteen hundred years or longer, and maybe there is something to that. More than a few restless Protestants have learned to swim the Tiber or make the pilgrimage to the Eastern Church.

The emerging church

Anything that is emerging is in process. It hasn't yet emerged, at least not fully. So hanging out with the emerging-church people was a little like getting in on the ground floor of a start-up tech company. You can be part of the cool, creative people who are so innovative they have to practice their specialties outside the big, bureaucratic corporations. Plus, the emerging church was offering a new (or at least a hip) perspective on being the people of God. Maybe I just needed a little jostling, a different perspective that might direct me to the right approach to the various church traditions. In hindsight, I give the emerging folks points for figuring out that the answer isn't banging your head into a wall looking for the perfect church.

House church

Abandon everything familiar and start over in somebody's living room, then try to not have all the problems other churches have. Good luck. And please tune your guitar before you lead the twelve people in a series of twenty-seven three-word praise choruses.

Media church

Join a church that networks its members through the Internet and broadcasts its services by video technology. Keep telling yourself this really is just like being with other Christians.

THE NEXT STOP ON GOD'S TOUR

Each of these options has advocates who write eloquent books and blogs pointing the rest of us to greener pastures. You might have made other stops that don't show up on my list. Like many of you, I took just about every one of those side roads on the journey, but I didn't find a stopping place, and I never bought the idea that trading up or moving to a new neighborhood would make much difference in the authentic Christian life I wanted to lead.

I did, however, find out why so many people leave the church completely while still holding on to some kind of spirituality. It isn't just because of their bad experiences. For many, it's because Jesus is leading them out of the church as they have known and experienced it. They find, after years of searching, that there is no solution to the church problem.

There is only one reliable constant. There is God, who is moving people out into the world. This is a Spirit-guided evolution of the movement Jesus started. It is a process of God moving Christians out of pews and toward the Kingdom that Jesus promised. And there is no predicting where that journey might take a person. But if it takes him or her outside organized Christianity, why would we argue with God about it?

God uses a surprising variety of things to move people, often in unexpected directions and to unexpected destinations. For many, the evolution leads to a Jesus-shaped spirituality that does not involve the church as they've experienced it in the past. It may take the form of a different church, a newly planted church, an alternative expression of church, or even, for some or for a season, of no recognizable church at all.

My mistake had been in assuming that Jesus was running a franchise operation, and I needed to discover which church was really his: pizza chain, hamburger chain, taco stand, coffee shop, or traditional diner. Which church business was he investing in right now? But on the contrary, Jesus is creating and bringing a Kingdom and doing it entirely on his own terms. Nobody has Jesus under contract to model their church's T-shirt.

When I finally abandoned the search for the real church and recognized that Jesus was leading people away from hidebound, rules-based religion, I was liberated. Jesus started a movement that was a dynamic, organic, evolving, and incredibly diverse body. Realizing this gave me a much different perspective on what the Holy Spirit was doing in the lives of Jesus-followers and in the world.

YOU CAN READ IT IN HIS BOOK

My journey to see the relationship of Jesus and the church began with Scripture. To start with, I looked at the New Testament again and realized that what I had always assumed was there—my church and all its baggage—wasn't there at all. It's time for us to take a closer look. (I'm not an agent from the denomination you left, armed with a guilt trip to arrest you and bring you back. I'm not trying to drag you into any church. I'm assuming that as a free and responsible adult, your journey will take you where you believe God wants you to be.)

The New Testament tells us Jesus' story four times, in the Gospels. Another book, Acts, gives us approximately forty years of history of some of the early Christians, beginning with Jesus' ascension back to God the Father. The New Testament then contains twenty-one letters of various kinds, all dealing with some aspect of being a Christian in the first century, and one book that describes a prophetic vision of spiritual reality, the book of Revelation. It is best described as a summary of the message of the whole Bible, told with a very loud soundtrack and state-of-the-art visuals.

The New Testament is quite a mash-up, but what holds all this material together? The obvious answer is Jesus Christ. But how does Jesus glue together the wild diversity of the New Testament?

One possible answer is that it's all held together, in one way or another, by the church itself. Look at the twenty-one letters: they are mostly written to or about churches or their leaders. The book of Acts records events in the early history of the church. The book of Revelation gives us a glimpse of the future triumph of God's church. So the glue that holds together all the material about Jesus is the church.

The next step is to find which church the New Testament is talking about and to join it. Right?

Not right.

When I was a kid, our church had a thirteen-point scorecard to help people answer the question, what church does the Bible identify as the church Jesus founded? You'll never guess which church always won that little quiz—our church. By some coincidence, we not only wrote the scorecard, we got all the answers right.

Here's another question: What is the relationship between Jesus and the church? The New Testament answer is that the church is visible evidence of the Holy Spirit constantly pointing to Jesus. Scripture doesn't just answer the question, what is the true church like? It also answers the question, what is the Holy Spirit doing these days?

Once you begin to see the church as part of what God is doing and not as a discount warehouse store, it's quite a wake-up call. For example, let me describe the church that shows evidence of the Holy Spirit in the community I've been part of for seventeen years. I'll describe it both as I see it and in New Testament terms.

There are thousands of Christians where I live. They express their faith through how they serve those in their families, through their work, in mercy ministries, in compassionate giving, and so forth. Christians saturate the fabric of our community. It's hard to escape them.

Many of these Christians attend or are members of congregations that are part of a larger, name-brand group (Methodist, Presbyterian, Lutheran, Episcopal, Catholic, United Church of Christ, Baptist, Assembly of God, Church of Christ, and so forth). Those churches preach, provide clothing and food, run schools, unite for prayer, do children's and youth ministries, and attend social events together. Other Christians who live in my town attend informal, nondenominational churches. These organized congregations—the name-brands we all recognize as well as the more informal ones—are important, but they are only one part of what God is doing.

A number of Christian schools operate in my town. Some are related to only one church, but most are supported by the contributions and work of many individuals and families. We have camps for children and youth sponsored by individuals and some churches. The town's youth center and a drug-treatment center are supported by individuals and churches. We have some Christian media, including a radio station, a television station, and a publishing operation.

We have faith-based medical clinics and Christians working in the medical arts. We have Christians in law enforcement and political life. We have Christians working throughout public education. In the part of the country where I live, Christians can openly bear witness to their faith as part of their work without fear of being hassled or appearing weird.

All of this—and much that I don't know about—is what the Holy Spirit is doing in my community. Together, this is the movement Jesus started as it is expressed in my neighborhood and community. It incorporates people who attend the same church their entire life and people who never enter a church. There are parts of the Christian community here that meet in comfortable, attractive facilities, and there are parts of the community that meet with two or three other people in a living room. There is a lot of diversity in this movement, but we all believe in Jesus, we believe the gospel, we pray and work for the Kingdom of God, and we look to the Holy Spirit to do all the things we can't do.

Among the people I have mentioned, there are some who sit in church and tell themselves they are the only true Christians. They may be right, but I doubt it. Others are so low-key that they fly solo or in small groups under God's direction. Some are leavers. They've had enough of church, but they haven't yet realized that God is leading them to another experience of himself. Some have left to care for aging parents, and some have left to go riding with a weekend motorcycle club. I'm not going to argue with them (or with you). For each person, it's a matter of responding to the Holy Spirit where you are in life and in the integrity of who God created you to be.

When you read the New Testament, you see there are good churches and not-so-good churches. There are people ministering to Jews and to Gentiles. There are people who find Jesus on their own and need to be taught about him. There are people sitting in church groups griping about how they are treated. There are some who may be the only Christians in their cities. There are churches Jesus threatens to put out of business.

There are churches made up of just a few people suffering in jail and churches of wealthy people getting drunk at the Lord's Supper.

There are organized churches and churches that are best described as controlled chaos. There are groups of people working for God's Kingdom, but they don't agree on basic things. There are arguments, teaching, and forgiveness.

WHAT GOD IS DOING

At the end of the day, Paul says it is his ambition to take the gospel where it's never been heard. Jesus says his Kingdom will replace the kingdoms of this world. Between the areas where "no one has heard" and the "Kingdom has come," God the Holy Spirit is doing countless things with different people at different places of spiritual maturity and with different degrees of success.

Jesus does what he does through people. They are in small groups or large; they disagree and agree; they get along or they don't. But Jesus' chosen method is to use people to get his work done. If you have left the church, are you still following Jesus, and are you still available to work in the Kingdom of God in this broken world? Are you open to the truth that in Jesus' Kingdom you still have an important part to play?

If you want to know what that noise is you're hearing, it's the angry mob that doesn't like hearing that the New Testament isn't just the story of their church. Those who support churchianity are using Jesus and the Scriptures to win an unnecessary argument. They feel it's their highest duty to prove the rightness of their chosen franchise operation. In fact, Christians have been so busy proving their wing of the church is number one with God that they fail to recognize the many ways God's Kingdom work is being done by those who are strikingly different from themselves. If you leave the franchised church, you might be going out the door to find God or to serve God more freely. Either way, it makes little difference to those who see Jesus only within the walls of a church building. In their minds, if you step outside you're wrong.

If you are a church-leaver, I don't want to drag you back. I have a better idea: find yourself in God's great and diverse purpose. Where do you fit in his movement, bringing the Kingdom of God to all people on earth? Can you find your place in the wide diversity of where God is working and how God is working? Can you replace churchianity with a Jesus-shaped spirituality that experiences God's power as God works toward fulfilling his incredible, history-changing purposes?

Wherever you are right now in relation to the church, you are still part of God's design for the Kingdom. Jesus is building his people and his movement his way. I believe we're all experiencing God's agenda for our lives. It's a journey of discovering a Jesus-shaped spirituality now and usefulness in God every day we're alive.

PART 3

THE JESUS LIFE

Living the Life Everyone Else Is Only Talking About

10

Jesus, the Bible,
and the Free-Range Believer

Yesterday morning I watched the baptism of one of the high school students I work with. She was an unlikely person to become a Jesus-follower, but that's one of the things I like about Jesus: he has a special place in his heart and in his plans for unlikely people. He often uses an outcast to change and bless the world.

This student has almost no background with Christianity. Her past is extremely broken and chaotic. She's a survivor who sees and hears in the Good News about Jesus a message of hope, love, and purpose for her life. It's exciting to think about where her life is going in the future.

Sometime this week I'm going to do something for her. I will do what I can to support her and mentor her in the future. But my plan for this week is to do something positively dangerous. Over time, this has proven to be explosive, controversial, and divisive.

I'm going to give her a Bible and tell her to read it. On her own. Not exclusively on her own, but yeah…on her own. When you read the Bible, you find out who Jesus really is. You can't read the New Testament and come out with Jesus the mushroom-snorting guru or Jesus the white, middle-class Republican.

Neither will you find a Protestant, churchgoing American. For those in the church who help sponsor the great Jesus Disconnect, it's bad news when new Christians start reading the Bible on their own. My young friend will surely discover that Jesus says radical things to his disciples about money, success, family, and the details of life. She will discover that Jesus signed no peace treaties with anyone's status quo or comfort zone, but he is unalterably determined that his Kingdom come on earth as it is in heaven, starting with her.

For those who want Jesus to be the passive, grinning poster boy for their superchurch, their save-America movement, or their pyramid-schemed God product, here is more bad news: My friend won't find any church denominations in the Bible. She won't find consumerism masking as discipleship. She won't find a chart detailing what kind of music to listen to or the proper clothes to wear. She won't be given a list of safe podcasts, radio stations, Web sites, and conferences.

Alister McGrath is one of the finest minds in the Christian world. An Oxford professor with a wide range of writing interests, he has exceptional credibility among a wide range of Christians. His recent book, *Christianity's Dangerous Idea,* says that the single most explosive claim after the resurrection of Jesus is that an individual can read and interpret the Bible for himself.[1] Not only is that true, but in Jesus-shaped spirituality, we count on the personal study of Scripture to be explosive. When I give a Bible to my young friend, that's exactly where we're starting: the dangerous idea of reading the Bible for yourself.

CHRISTIANS WHO OPPOSE READING THE BIBLE

I can already smell the gunpowder. "You can't let a new Christian make her own assumptions about what the Bible means. It's not responsible to let her pick and choose what she likes and what she doesn't like in the Bible." I'm well aware that my friend will need help in her exploration of the Bible. She'll need to be taught what the Bible is and what kind of literature she's reading. She'll need an introduction to the parameters and methods of right interpretation. She needs to read and discuss the Bible with other Christians. Yes, she needs to seek out good Bible teachers. All that in good time and in its place.

You see, all of us who believe that the Bible is our primary source of information about Jesus have to make a decision about how much we trust God to speak to individual Christians through the Bible. McGrath rightly points out that it's the classic Protestant-Catholic divide, the reformers' insistence on sola fide and sola scriptura versus the Roman church's reliance on the Scriptures plus church tradition plus the magisterial authority of the church. But I'd contend that in recent decades, long after Martin Luther's ninety-five theses, that evangelical Protestants have been busy taking the Bible away from individual Christians in favor of indoctrinating new converts with the party line of a particular church denomination.

In place of the Bible, evangelical Christianity has vested authority in celebrity preachers, PowerPoint presentations, substitute narratives, resolutions passed at denominational conventions, and allegiance to a preferred doctrinal strain (Wesleyan, Reformed, Anabaptist, Anglican, Lutheran, Free Church, Pentecostal, and so forth). Don't let all the new Bible translations fool you into thinking the chain has been removed from the pulpit edition of the Scriptures.

To be honest, the presence of the Bible in many churches is optional. To some it's a downright hassle, so they pump up their Bible substitutes. To keep you from having to read it on your own, the Bible will be read and explained to you by the church's official custodians, or it won't be read at all because knowledge of its content is assumed, or it will be fed to you through some other medium. I've seen preachers show a film clip and then say, "Now in the Bible somewhere it says..." I'm waiting for that preacher to end his rambling with "Trust me, O sheep. Just trust me." I'll say, "No thanks."

I would propose that Jesus-shaped spirituality undertakes a dramatically different approach to the Bible. A faithful Christian should be suspicious of those who want to confine the reading and study of the Bible to the authoritarian class. And we need to be careful around those who rework the Bible through the latest high-tech medium. If the teacher is not teaching from a substantial text, rooting what he or she teaches securely in the Bible's focus on Jesus, then a Christian should be suspicious of the teaching. I don't mean half a verse here and two-thirds of a verse there, where Scripture is manipulated to fit the speaker's alliterative four-point sermon. A teaching that's aimed at the conscience needs to be based on a text with some substance and scope so that the meaning of the Scripture emerges without being filtered through the grid and the pet doctrines of the official interpretation squad.

In other words, if they don't want you reading your Bible to find Jesus as the heart of the matter, you should be suspicious and resistant. You have my permission to raise a lot of questions, even if it annoys them.

HOW THE CHURCH TRIES TO SILENCE GOD

Wait, I see that hand. "What you're suggesting is fraught with danger. It's irresponsible to let anyone come to their own conclusions about what the Bible says without the supervision of those who have been trained in ancient Greek and Hebrew."

One of the most interesting discussions I have moderated at my Web site, InternetMonk.com, was on the subject of Bible distribution. Every year I try to distribute Bibles to all the students I minister to, and I am involved with distributing the Bible in India and elsewhere through ministries I support. I believe it is an unqualified good for people to have the Bible in their own language and to read it on their own.

Amazingly, many Christians—Protestant, Catholic, and Orthodox—who discussed this matter on my Web site disagreed that it's always good to get the Bible into people's hands. There was a remarkable amount of hand-wringing about what might happen if Billy or Ahmed were to start reading a Bible without proper guidance. How could you ensure that Billy or Ahmed arrived at acceptable conclusions?

I understand the concern for all to avoid damning error, and I can cite examples of the hazards and consequences when zealots create a false religion and swear it is God-breathed. But the greater good has to be the dynamic of God, one person, and the text of Scripture. What do we believe is happening and can happen in that dynamic? Inside or outside the church, when an individual reads the Bible and is genuinely looking for God and God's truth, doesn't the Holy Spirit respond by speaking to that person? Does God speak to us—both open-hearted believers and seeking nonbelievers—through the Bible? Or is his ability to teach us limited only to the times when we are hearing from a trained Bible teacher?

Allowing a reader to seek God in the Bible, freely and without an escort, poses some risk. But there is a greater risk in gluing the pages together so that no one can read God's Word unless a certified authority is present to manage the process. Who are church leaders trying to protect—the individual reader who might misread a statement in the Bible or the customs of American evangelicalism that have borrowed as much from Thomas Jefferson's Declaration of Independence as they have from Jesus' Sermon on the Mount?

Think about it. What pastor who is up to his ears in leading a capital campaign wants parishioners walking up and asking why the church is planning to build a multimillion-dollar facility when Jesus told the rich young ruler to sell all that he had and give it to the poor? One of the reasons we don't have a Jesus-shaped spirituality is the conspiracy among successful pastors to keep displaying only the tame parts of the Bible on the overhead screen. We have been placing our trust in church leaders who have a vested interest in maintaining the status quo, not in telling us all that God has to say.

Let's say a majority of the members of the city council own stock in a paving company. When the time comes for city streets to be resurfaced, bids are put out. The council then votes on the leading bids, and a majority of the members votes for the paving company the council members own stock in. If most evangelical pastors were members of a city council, controlling the information that gets out and rigging the system to ensure the outcome they desire, you'd say they had a conflict of interest.

It's time to stop supporting a rigged system. The cost of allowing the gatekeepers to determine what is taught and what is overlooked is much too high.

Churchianity, which is the height of status-quo religion, is a far cry from Jesus-shaped spirituality. In this country prior to 1865, preachers read Bible verses on slavery but failed to ask if Jesus approved of buying and selling human beings. To this day, preachers read the story of Jesus and the woman at the well, they read the book of Esther, they read about Priscilla and Dorcas and the women who arrived first at the empty tomb, while allowing (and even encouraging or demanding) women to be limited to filling secondary roles in the church. They gladly turn a blind eye to the full import of Jesus' liberation of women.

So I'll give a Bible to my student who recently was baptized in an act of affirming her new faith in Jesus. And I'll encourage her to read the Bible on her own. I'll suggest she ask questions as they occur to her, even the hardest questions that are likely to arise. The cost of doing anything else is too high.

When church officials tell curious, inquisitive minds to stop asking troublesome questions, our faith is in jeopardy.

FREE TO ALL: THE INVITATION TO LISTEN TO GOD

Think what would happen if we allowed just anybody to read the Bible and search for what God is saying to them. We may wind up with Pentecostals praying for corpses to be resurrected at the funeral home. We might find that Appalachian snake handlers multiply like flies at a church picnic. We could see several thousand new, combative denominations spring up, and the very real possibility that someone, somewhere, might circulate an erroneous biblical teaching. They might even put it on the Internet.

We'd run the risk of having a few more heretics in the world, and it all may get rather messy. (Of course, heretics can also spring from the ranks of those who never read the Bible. But that's not the focus of this discussion.) If you don't like the possibility that an individual reading the Bible without close supervision might misconstrue some of the things he reads, I have an alternative. I can give you a list of churches where the idea that you hear God when you read Scripture is completely off-limits.

The choice is ours. We can give in to centralized church control, or we can take the risk of seeking God as he reveals himself in his Word. We can enjoy the freedom of meeting with God while reading the Bible on our own, and we can ask him to lead us and teach us.

My Roman Catholic friends often point out the advantages of having a pope and a magisterium who settle all doctrinal issues. I generally answer with this: Do you prefer one man claiming infallibility telling you what the Bible says, or twenty thousand very fallible people who are reading the Bible and looking to be corrected by its truth? Yeah, it's a messy imitation of a circus sometimes, but I prefer the circus.

Jesus-shaped spirituality takes the risk of letting people seek God without constant supervision. It is not Jesus-shaped if we hide Jesus behind those who are working overtime to keep everything safe, middle class, and comfortable. Sure, reading the Bible on your own is dangerous. But who really wants the other option—a bland, neutered, toothless Jesus who is kept on a leash to preside over a convenient, culturally correct spirituality? Some of the worst episodes in history resulted from that system. I'd advise you to pass.

Does this mean that we leave people entirely to their own reading of the Bible so they can draw their own conclusions? No, it doesn't mean we leave them there, but I think we have to trust God enough to allow the Holy Spirit to speak directly to individuals from the Scripture without requiring them to submit in advance to a mandatory interpretation. The fear that someone will follow a verse of Scripture out of the safety zone and into error has paralyzed entire communities of Christians. And the biblical notion that the Holy Spirit might prompt a person while reading Scripture terrifies large numbers of evangelicals. The Holy Spirit is great in theory, but when he starts actually doing things, you never know when the situation might get out of control.

I live in an area of Appalachia that could be called "religiously primitive," to be kind. The churches are reflections of mountain culture. The clergy seldom have a day of education past high school. Their theology is unsophisticated. The expressions of Christian faith that I hear in sermons, songs, and testimonies would not impress the highly educated custodians of polished orthodoxy.

It has always struck me, however, that in the midst of much theological ignorance and error, there is always a remarkably strong Jesus-shaped direction to what I hear in this mountain culture. For example, suffering and faithfulness in the midst of poverty are embraced. The economics of Jesus are here, as are the biblical warnings to the rich. Forgiveness of those who have hurt you is a frequent message, and utter dependence on God to provide, guide, and rescue is a constant message as well. Over and over, we hear about the need to love one another. Love for other Christians is abundant, and the union of faith and works in a healthy Christian life is demonstrated constantly.

But if you're looking for an erudite treatise on justification by faith as the doctrine is expressed in the various views of the sacraments, you're in for a long wait. You won't find an abundance of theologically savvy sermons in the more remote reaches of Appalachia. You will, however, find the simplicity of the gospel and the straightforward preaching of Jesus' words.

I am not defending the misuse or the abuse of Scripture. Ignorance of the truth that God has revealed is hurtful to individuals and churches alike, whether they are wealthy and suburban or poverty stricken and way off the beaten path. I am saying, however, that these faithful people, with their Bibles and without the confining hand of official church structures telling them what to believe, make a remarkable witness to Jesus-shaped spirituality. In that department, they go well beyond any flock of theologians or discernment police I've encountered in more "respectable" settings.

I believe I can trust the Holy Spirit. I want the gifts of the Spirit that guide the church to guide my young friend as she reads the Bible. I don't want her to join a cult or start one, but I am content to let her begin her adventure of following Jesus with the confidence that her openness to the Spirit speaking in the Word of God is basic. I don't believe the Spirit has signed an exclusive contract with any denomination, seminary, or ministry to which my student must report. While she needs other Christians to guide her rightly in the Bible, she doesn't need them in the same way she needs the Holy Spirit to speak to her.

As we will see in a later chapter, I believe in the importance of Christian community and the ministry of that community to provide boundaries and definition to spiritual growth and healthy spirituality. I mourn, however, the loss of our openness to the voice of the Holy Spirit directing us in new and important Jesus-shaped directions. It is rare to find an established community of Christians that encourages radical expressions of following Jesus. The natural conservatism of institutions is deeply rooted in the desire to survive, and that desire colors and limits the way they read the Bible and how they see God functioning in the world.

HEARING THE HOLY SPIRIT

Whether you stand inside the church or are on the outside, I wouldn't be at all surprised if you, like Martin Luther King Jr. did in a Birmingham jail, wonder how the established church ever became so conservative that the voice of the Spirit can't find a foothold. To all who have left the church but not the faith, my appeal is simple: Listen to the Spirit in the Scripture! Ask what it is that God is saying.

One of my favorite stories in the Bible is Peter's vision of ritually unclean animals being lowered from heaven on a huge sheet. The animals were mentioned in the Old Testament book of Leviticus as absolutely forbidden for any Jew to eat. But Jesus declared all foods clean.[2] Peter, of course, was invested in reading the Bible the way his mama and his pastor had taught him to read it. So the Holy Spirit gave Peter a vision—a repeated vision, in fact—during a nap. Peter saw a sheet covered with unclean animals, such as pigs and lobsters. They were being lowered from heaven. Then the Holy Spirit told Peter to eat!

Imagine this. God's Spirit was commanding a follower of Jesus to do something that, according to everything Peter had been taught, was forbidden to the children of God. You talk about a dilemma.

If Peter had run down to his local church and asked for assistance in understanding what God was saying, he almost certainly would have been told that he was mistaken. He must have heard God wrong, or maybe he simply mistook a nightmare for a vision from God. The preacher would have insisted that the Leviticus passages had to be taken as God's settled and uncompromised command to ensure that his people are different from other nations. The Jews do not eat unclean animals, and under no circumstances would God ever contradict Scripture.

Peter wasn't a man without strong biases and prejudices in this area. He felt a lot more comfortable supporting the Jewish bias against Gentiles—the "unclean people"—than he did considering Paul's insistence that in Christ there is no Jew or Gentile. Jesus had told Peter and the other apostles that the Holy Spirit would lead them into all truth. Jesus had told Peter that there were "other sheep" who needed to come to the great Shepherd.[3] So the dream involving unclean animals was not the first time Peter had encountered a bold challenge to the old idea of uncleanness.

Peter had learned from Jesus to listen for what the Spirit of God might do that was very different from what Peter and the other disciples had always been taught. Peter, after seeing the vision of the unclean animals and being commanded to eat, got the message. He preached the gospel to a Roman soldier's household and baptized his entire family. As you think about that, realize that the soldier and his family were completely outside the circle of acceptability to a practicing Jew. They were Gentiles, the "unclean people" whom Peter had always been taught to avoid.

But Jesus changed everything. The Holy Spirit applying the truth of Scripture to one person, in this case Peter, is what made the message clear for the whole church.

The impact of Peter's vision and his subsequent obedience to God is still felt today. The vast majority of people around the world who will ever believe in Jesus owe it partially to Peter's vision of the sheet full of animals. It was an inexplicable encounter with the Holy Spirit totally outside the bounds of safe church teaching. It was an experience with God that got through to Peter and helped form his Jesus-shaped life.

I'm not suggesting that God will send visions to everyone or that every vision is as revolutionary or as world changing as Peter's. The apostles were in a unique position, but over and over again, I hear about God's Spirit lifting the Word of God out of safe, church-regulated venues and using it to change and empower people. God shakes off the dusty interpretations and applies his Word in fresh, new ways to unreached places and people. How desperately we need that kind of prayerful, expectant Bible hearing today!

Even with all the risks that are involved in giving one brand-new Christian a Bible, the risks are worth it. So go ahead, all you free-range Christians. Open up the ammo. Let's blow something up. Like the safe, expected idea of the Christian life.

11

It's a Bad Idea
to Be a Good Christian

In a classic Bugs Bunny cartoon, there arose the following verbal diagnosis on the part of Bugs as he discussed with Daffy Duck when and whom should be shot: "Hmm...pronoun trouble!"[1]

I would like to offer my humble analysis of the gaps and omissions in a great deal of evangelical Christianity. My initial diagnosis is this: "Hmm...adjective trouble!"

Christians and their adjectives. They can cause a lot of trouble.

An adjective modifies a noun. It takes a simple person, place, or thing, and by adding its adjectival magic, can create something far more interesting.

A dog is one thing. A rabid dog is another. A rabid dog biting your leg is a matter of enough concern to set down your coffee and seek assistance.

There's the church. Then there's the dynamic, seeker-sensitive church with a kickin' worship band.

There's worship. Add an adjective, and it's emerging worship. Or extreme worship, Spirit-led worship, or ancient-future worship.

Adjectives. They do change things, don't they? Sometimes they help, but at other times they obscure the plain meaning of what needs to be said. When it comes to Christianity, it's a good idea to put adjectives on probation and admit them into active service only after they have proven they will be an asset.

Why? Because dedication to the wrong adjectives has been costly to the cause of Christianity. I'll give you a few egregious examples:

- The "victorious" Christian life. Is there any other kind?
- A "good" Christian witness. Should any of us aspire to a bad Christian witness?
- "Dynamic" worship. Don't get me started.
- "Anointed" preaching. I don't see any oil on the preacher's head, unless it's Vitalis.
- The "true" church. Where is the synthetic church, the cloned church, or the "aliens stole my church"?
- "Extreme" youth ministry. Have Christians abused any other adjective as much as this one?
- "Really" saved. It's like being pregnant. You either are or you're not. You can't be a little bit saved.

The adjectival problem is not just something that's interesting to talk about. It's an unnecessary distraction from the gospel and the work of God's Kingdom. The characteristics we just listed—experiencing victory, witnessing to Christ's love and grace, worshiping God, and so forth—summarize the components of the Christian life. They need no adornment. But the unthinking habit of Christians to stick on the typical adjectives has taken one thing and turned it into another.

When I talk to those who have left the church or are preparing to, I often find that it's not the Christian faith that rings false in their ears. It's the qualifications and conditions that are forced onto the experience of faith. The accepted adjectives send large numbers of believers in a very different direction—often out the church's doors.

It's not enough to just be a church member. You have to be a "faithful" church member, meaning you're there every time the lights go on. Guess who got to beatify the faithful church members and inflict guilt on everyone else? I don't remember anyone taking a congregational vote on that one.

You can't be just a Christian. You're required to be a "spiritual" Christian, and if you're not, you'll be lumped in with the "carnal" Christians. We've stuck so many adjectives on the front of the word *Christian* that it has lost most of its meaning. These days you have to name your tribe— reformed, fundamentalist, creedal, progressive, nondenominational, Jesus-shaped, and so forth. We've reached the point where we don't know what to think of another believer unless we have an adjective to guide us. Atheists do better than we do at seeing all Christians equally.

For me, the real damage was done with two of the most common adjectives used by Christians. They are the "victorious" Christian life and the necessity of being a "good" Christian. If we believe Jesus is Lord, then isn't the Christian life victorious by design? And what's a good Christian? Jesus said there is none good, only the Father.

The message of the Christian obsession with adjectives is clear. While most of us are living a merely Christian life, out there somewhere are the blessed persons who have discovered something else. They possess something that's not ordinary, something on a higher level. They have laid hold of the "victorious" Christian life, which makes them "good" Christians.

IT'S HARD TO MANUFACTURE VICTORY

Soon after I committed my life to Christ, this sort of thing just about pushed me over the edge. Preachers preached about victorious Christians and song lyrics celebrated it. Book titles promised it in a few easy steps. Some people would stand up and give a testimony: "I'm living it! I'm living the victorious Christian life!" They, of course, were good Christians.

But what about me? I felt like a regular, run-of-the-mill Christian. How could I be victorious and not just ordinary?

I did my best to follow what the preacher said on Sunday mornings. I had accepted Jesus into my heart and prayed the recommended prayer. I'd made a public profession of faith and been baptized. I had a Bible. I came to church. I prayed...a little. I tried to be a good witness, but I could plainly see that I wasn't living the "victorious" life.

I was still a lot like I was before I became a Christian. I had the same sins, the same habits, and the same problems. What was wrong?

Whenever I'd ask about it, the answers were always the same. I hadn't "totally surrendered." I hadn't "given all." I wasn't "trusting God" completely. I needed to have an "intimate" and powerful "daily time with God." I wasn't praying in the will of God.

I grew up attending a church that followed in the revivalist tradition. The preacher insisted that we have constant experiences of and encounters with God, so the weekly exhortation was always, "Are you sure you are a fully surrendered Christian? Are you living in total victory over sin? Have you done everything you can to be the best Christian you can be?"

Measured by this standard, I was a miserable failure. A loser with a capital *L*. As more qualifiers and conditions were stuck on to what it meant to be a Christian, the worse it became for me. I had never gone a day without sinning, or even ten minutes. To make it even worse, the full responsibility to ramp up a victorious Christian life fell squarely on me, not on Christ and the transforming power of the gospel. The preaching I heard every Sunday reminded me that God would help me out only after I did all the right things. (But why would I need his help if I could manage, completely on my own, to do everything right?)

I concluded that either I wasn't living the Christian life or someone wasn't telling the truth. I'd give it my best shot, trying even harder to get started right in living the Christian life. I'd fail again. Then I'd begin again, making big promises and resolutions. This time I'd really get on top of things. My seesaw approach to being a Christian was an every-week event. One more prayer, one more trip to the altar, one more big experience at a revival meeting, one more surrender or dramatic religious experience.

CHRISTIANS WHO LIKE PENTECOST

Then I ran into some Pentecostal and charismatic Christians at school. I noticed that when I saw them in the cafeteria, they would always smile at me. Later I found out why. It was because they were living the "victorious" Christian life. At least that's what they said.

These guys had a plan. They even had a shortcut. It involved only three steps:

1. Pray for the baptism in the Holy Spirit.
2. Get it.
3. Speak in tongues.

That was it. Three things, and there you go.

Add to this fast start the advice to hang out with other Pentecostals and charismatics and do what they do: things like casting out demons, claiming miracles (even when the best empirical evidence said otherwise), raising your hands in worship, calling on God to do dramatic things, and so on.

I was up for this. If the Baptists didn't know how to really get the "victorious" adjective in front of the Christian life, I could rely on these smiling people to do it. They had a direct power line to the Almighty, and all I had to do was tap into it with a sincere prayer.

One night a bunch of charismatics took me and a friend to their church on an off night, got us down to the altar, prayed over us, and called on God to baptize us in the Holy Spirit and give us the gift of tongues. It was just us, them, and God.

This was the easiest thing I'd ever done. I took right off speaking in tongues as I'd been instructed. I had Jesus on the main line. At long last I had laid hold of the victorious Christian life. All I had to do was plug in my new experience of speaking in tongues, and then I'd be victorious.

This was a far cry from the Baptist approach. The Baptists were all for getting victorious by way of attending two or three revival meetings a year. But why wait around for the next scheduled revival when you can get victory the Pentecostal way, through the baptism of the Spirit and speaking in tongues? (I was on board with this, but to most Baptists such things were viewed as something akin to joining the Baha'is.)

My charismatic phase revealed three things to me. First, I was excellent at mimicking whatever religious behavior was going on around me, including speaking in tongues. I'm still pretty good at it, and it has been decades since I've been even a trifling charismatic.

Second, I was no more victorious as a tongues-speaker than I was before, but my new religious community supplied more pressure to act spiritual, and I complied. Their way to be spiritual was a lot easier, since the demonstrable evidences were more up-front. A person uttering unintelligible sounds is pretty hard not to observe, after all.

But sadly all my efforts to manufacture a victorious Christian life were taking me further away from a fundamental truth of the life of faith. I was turning my faith into a farce, and whenever I got tired of being a religious liar, I'd have to face up to the truth.

This was ironic, because before I became a Christian, I was quite good at pointing out the hypocritical phoniness of the Christians around me, especially some of the high-profile ones. Now, as a freshly minted Pentecostal, I was becoming the very thing I had once hated: a phony believer, conning my new Pentecostal friends as the price for acceptance into their group.

THE GOSPEL WITHOUT ADJECTIVES

After I rattled around on this path for a few years, I knew I needed to recalibrate my life with the real Jesus. I had to ask myself a question: Was the Christian life actually the "victorious" Christian life I was faking? Was it supposed to be vibrant, electric, dynamic, supernatural, awesome, and _____? (Insert your adjective of choice.) Or was the Christian life different? simpler? more honest?

This journey led me toward the discoveries that I will be sharing in the next few chapters. The Christian life is an expression of the gospel. If your preferred gospel is *Your Best Life Now,* then your Christian life will be something like "discovering your awesome, unique destiny."

If your gospel is "God wants you to have a dynamic experience every day!" then your Christian life will be a constant amusement park of dramatic divine interventions.

If your gospel is "Jesus Christ is our salvation. He gives life to those who come to him by faith," then your Christian life will look like the joy of the rescued and the humility of the undeservedly graced.

If your gospel is "Jesus is for losers, and there's no need to lie about it," then your Christian life will be "Hello. My name is Michael, and I'm a big sinner with a bigger Savior."

Martin Luther let me know that I was not qualified to receive the victorious-Christian-life merit badge. He also let me know that I wasn't a very good Christian. I'd been reading the reformer's works in a course taught by Dr. Timothy George, one of the finest church historians of our time. I found out then what the gospel is.

The gospel that put an end to the proud monk Martin Luther and produced a Christian created one of the few mystical experiences of my life. That gospel laid itself out in my mind and heart in a way I'd never seen it or heard it before. I wrote several pages of notes describing the explosion of truth that overwhelmed me that day, but I've lost the notes. The memory of Timothy George's lecture, however, is still vivid in my mind and faith today.

For the first time, the truth that Jesus is the one Mediator between God and human beings[2] knocked me to the floor and suspended me over the truth that God had done all things necessary for my salvation. I could stop looking for the secret key, and I could ditch the quest to demonstrate that I was a Christian hero. I was humbled as I looked at a universe of grace that filled my empty soul with the love of God in Jesus.

He did it all. He traversed the separation. He brought together the unreconcilable. He had paid the debt and had become the necessary sacrifice. He had loved me to the uttermost. He had given all this to me as a gift. I had nothing to offer, nothing to contribute, nothing to do but simply stop ignoring his gift and receive it. I was a drowning man whose rescue depended on stopping all efforts to swim and trusting Someone who was not going to make me a better swimmer, but who would drown in my place.

This experience did more than give me a racing heartbeat. It demolished the idea that I could be anything other than what I was: a broken, sinful, wounded, failing, hurting human being. To try to become something else was an affront to God's love for me. To try to make myself presentable or acceptable made me less capable of receiving the simple gift of Jesus' mediation on my behalf.

Jesus was not clearing the road so I could ride victoriously through life. He was becoming the road that would carry me through all the garbage, falls, failures, and disasters that were the inevitable results of my existence. In trying to make myself lovable, I had been distancing myself from true love. In pretending to be a leading candidate for the religious life, I was abandoning the life of grace. In seeking to be a good Christian, I was deserting the truth that there is no gospel for "good" Christians, because the Lamb of God was nailed to an altar for those who are not good and who are no good at pretending to be good.

WHEN CHRISTIAN ADJECTIVES LIE

I discovered, while listening to a lecture on Luther's breakthrough discovery of grace, that the victorious Christian life is a lie. It is a completely un-Jesus-shaped imposter. The Christian life isn't a denial of the prodigal son parable, with the prodigal suddenly becoming a good boy and making his father proud. It is lived at the point where the empty-handed, thoroughly humbled son kneels before his father and has nothing to offer. The son can do nothing but be loved. He is empty and has only one recourse—receive the gift of all things and eternity.

The exhausting effort to be a good Christian denies Christ. If you insist on securing your own holiness and acceptability, you disqualify yourself from receiving anything from Jesus. He came to earth to save sinners, not good Christians.

This discovery, like most Jesus-shaped discoveries, doesn't go over well in your usual religious environments. It plays well in AA meetings, counselors' offices, bars, and prison chapels, but doesn't fit the program in the success seminars and motivational sessions passing as mainstream North American evangelicalism. It falls far short of the glamorous lifestyles of wealth, beauty, and popularity that keep showing up in church promos. It is, however, very good news to the poor, the brokenhearted, and the destitute, who welcome the message that Jesus proclaimed and lived.

If you have left the church or are headed for the door, there is a strong possibility that you have to leave in order to hold on to your integrity. You realized you can no longer play the religion game. You may be playing other games—I'm not letting any of us off the hook. But you found you could no longer be party to the endless act that says you are living the victorious Christian life.

If that is the case, your leaving in order to find true humanity, real vulnerability, and surprising grace may be the greatest gift you could give to the church. Not because of your absence, but because you have become one more person who has chosen real life in place of the inauthenticity of pretending to have it all together.

In 1521 Martin Luther wrote a letter to his friend and fellow reformer Philipp Melanchthon. Melanchthon was the type of person who tormented himself over his sins. In his letters to Luther, Melanchthon would rehearse his struggles to the point of irritating Luther and reminding him of his days as a monk with a magnifying-glass conscience.

In one famous letter, Luther decided to shock Melanchthon with a bit of hyperbole.

> If you are a preacher of grace, then preach a true and not a ficti-
> tious grace; if grace is true, you must bear a true and not a ficti-
> tious sin. God does not save people who are only fictitious
> sinners. Be a sinner and sin boldly, but believe and rejoice in
> Christ even more boldly, for he is victorious over sin, death, and
> the world. As long as we are here [in this world] we have to sin.
> This life is not the dwelling place of righteousness, but, as Peter
> says, we look for new heavens and a new earth in which right-
> eousness dwells. It is enough that by the riches of God's glory we
> have come to know the Lamb that takes away the sin of the
> world. No sin will separate us from the Lamb, even though we
> commit fornication and murder a thousand times a day. Do you
> think that the purchase price that was paid for the redemption of
> our sins by so great a Lamb is too small? Pray boldly—you too
> are a mighty sinner.[3]

I'm sure that Luther understood something religious people often misunderstand, something that is clear in the Bible: grace is shocking. It's a
stunning reversal of the way the world does business. It offends the moral
calculus of those who want religion to be a way to force their children into
good behavior. It overturns the tables and blows the minds of those who
want God to be a cosmic police officer, writing tickets to the speeders.

Grace, when rightly understood, is an even greater shock to those
who prefer to see Christianity as a way to put the well-behaved, the
blessed, and the righteous on the cover of the latest issue of *Worldly Success* magazine. If you want God to reward your efforts to be good by making you "the successful Christian," grace will let you down. That is the
unexpected surprise of God's grace.

JESUS WEIGHS IN ON "GOOD CHRISTIANS"

In the tenth chapter of Mark, Jesus, who is on the way to his death, hears a stunning request made by two of his clueless disciples: "We want you to do for us whatever we ask of you."[4]

James and John had bought into too many lying adjectives. They were deceived by the lies of competition and status and believed in a false pecking order in God's Kingdom. Instead of living in the truth of "whoever would be first among you must be slave of all,"[5] they were sold on the religious pride of "I'm closer to Jesus than you are." In today's language, they were striving to be, not just good Christians, but the best Christians.

Even though we know that James and John incurred the displeasure of the other ten disciples,[6] most evangelical Christians still catch a ride on the "good Christian" bandwagon. We consider ourselves good and maybe even a little bit superior because we hang out with Jesus. We assume that when God comes through, he'll give us what we want.

This one was too big for Jesus to let slide. At first he played along with James and John after they asked him to do whatever they wanted. He asked what they wanted. Their answer? When you become king of Israel, we want to be your right- and left-hand men. In other words, we want the power, the influence, the goods, and the payoff for sticking with you for three demanding years.

Ironically, this conversation comes after Jesus had predicted his own suffering, death, and resurrection. We're a lot like James and John, pursuing the life of following Jesus in terms of what's in it for us. Jesus tries to get us to understand that he is dying for us; meanwhile we're asking him how to parlay our obedience into some good times and bling.

Jesus asks the two disciples: "Are you able to suffer, even to die with me?" "Sure," they are quick to reply. "No problem."

If this story weren't so close to describing our own spiritual blindness and self-righteousness, we could read it with some distance. But we can't be critical of James and John because we'd have to judge ourselves in the same breath. Jesus is extending costly grace, purchased with his own crucified body and broken heart, and we're looking for a way to make his sacrifice pay off.

We don't see that the powerful changes that happen in the life of a disciple never come from the disciple working hard at doing anything. They come from arriving at a place where Jesus is everything, and we are simply overwhelmed with the gift. Sometimes it seems as if God loves us too much. His love goes far beyond our ability to stop being moral, religious, obedient, and victorious, and we just collapse in his arms.

Out of the gospel that Jesus is the only Mediator between God and humanity[7] comes a Christian life that looks like Jesus, a life Jesus would recognize. It's a life that looks like Jesus, because Jesus does everything, and all we do is accept his gift. And to accept his gift, we have to give up trying to be Jesus.

Out of that discovery comes a Christian life that is free from the tyranny of unnecessary adjectives—even my preferred modifier, *Jesus-shaped*—and simply follows after the One who loves us beyond words or repayment. Out of that grace comes a Christian life that is impossible to explain, even to ourselves, except to say:

> I have been crucified with Christ. It is no longer I who live, but
> Christ who lives in me. And the life I now live in the flesh I live
> by faith in the Son of God, who loved me and gave himself for
> me. I do not nullify the grace of God, for if righteousness were
> through the law, then Christ died for no purpose.[8]

It's now time to look at the Jesus-shaped Christian life, first for its essential qualities and then with the question, What produces a Jesus-shaped disciple?

When I Am Weak

T he voice on the other end of the phone told a story that has become so familiar I could almost have finished it from the third sentence. An admired Christian leader, carrying the secret burden of depression, had finally broken under the crushing load of holding it all together.

As prayer networks in our area began to make calls and send e-mails, the same questions were asked again and again: How could this happen? How could someone who spoke so confidently of God, someone whose life gave such evidence of Jesus' presence, come to the point of a complete breakdown? How can someone who has the answers for everyone else have no answers for himself?

Indeed. After all the confident talk of new life, new creation, the power of God, healing, wisdom, miracles, the power of prayer…why are we so weak? Why do so many "good Christians" turn out to be just like everyone else? Divorced. Depressed. Broken. Full of pain and secrets. Addicted, needy, and phony.

And there is the big assumption that lies behind all these questions: "I thought we were different."

It's remarkable, considering the tone of so many sermons, that any church has honest people show up at all. I can't imagine that any religion in history has made as many false claims and promises as evangelical Christians make any day of the week. Christians somehow feel compelled to stretch the truth in their quest to say that Jesus "makes us better people right now." With constant promises of joy, power, contentment, healing, prosperity, purpose, better relationships, successful parenting, and freedom from every kind of affliction, I wonder why more Christians aren't either being sued for false advertising or hauled off to a psych ward to be examined for serious delusions.

Evangelicals love to hear testimonies of how screwed up the testifier *used to be.* They aren't interested in hearing about how screwed up the person is today. But the fact is, we're screwed up. Then, now, all the time in between and, it's safe to assume, the rest of the time we're alive on earth. But Christians will pay a lot of money to hear a Bible teacher tell them they are only a few prayers, Bible verses, and sermon CDs away from being a lot better.

Please, call this off. I'm seeing, in my life and the lives of others, a full-on commitment to lying about our condition. It's absolutely pathological. Evangelicals expressed moral outrage when Bill Clinton tried to cloud the issue of his misdeeds by stating: "It depends upon what the meaning of the word *is* is."[1] President Clinton is considered a world-champion liar, right? This is the same man who told the nation on network television: "I did not have sexual relations with that woman, Miss Lewinsky."[2] But he clearly *did* have sexual relations with Miss Lewinsky. If you saw the presidential denial, you knew he was lying.

Those who recall the Clinton years are nodding in agreement. But how many nodding Christians have a pile of garbage sitting in the middle of their lives? How many of us are addicted to food, pornography, the Internet, shopping, fishing, golf, money? How many of us are depressed, angry, unforgiving, and just plain mean? How many of us are a walking, talking course on basic hypocrisy, because we can't look at ourselves in the mirror and admit we are a collection of brokenness? How many of us are willing to admit, out loud, that we became the broken people that we are while we called ourselves "good Christians" who want to witness to others about God's power to transform lives?

If you have your Bible handy, look something up for me. Review the stories of the leading heroes in Scripture, and tell me which ones weren't screwed up. Don't the seriously flawed people—such as Abraham, Jacob,

Moses, David, and Hosea—outnumber the "good Christians" by about ten to one? And isn't it true that the closer we look at a biblical character, the more likely it will be that we'll see a whole nasty collection of things that Christians say they no longer have to deal with?

To hear Christians tell it, they have overcome things that Israel's greatest king—the man after God's own heart—never got on top of because, praise God, they've been fixed. We're not talking about a few temper tantrums or small lies but big stuff like violence, sex addictions, abusive behavior, deceit, and depression. It's all there, yet we still listen to a preacher who flops open a Bible on the pulpit before he talks about "Ten Ways to Have Joy That Never Goes Away!"

Where is the laugh track?

WHAT ABOUT HOLINESS AND SANCTIFICATION?

You might want to interrupt me here to talk about sanctification. It's a biblical word and a recurring theme in Scripture. According to most of the teaching you'll hear from evangelical preachers, sanctification is the gradual process of becoming not just positionally righteous in Christ but experientially righteous in daily life. It is the process of spiritual growth and maturity in which God gives a believer a new heart and makes the believer a new person in Christ. And this is not just figurative speech but a measureable, quantifiable, verifiable improvement in speech, behavior, attitude, thoughts, and Christian commitment. "We're getting better. I've been delivered!"

I'm sure you've heard that working definition, and I don't use the term *working* by accident. But it's not true to the message of the gospel or the consistent teaching of the New Testament. In a sense, I suppose some of us are getting better. For instance, my scary temper is better than it used to be. Of course, the reason my temper is better is that in the process of cleaning up the messes I've made with my temper, I've discovered about twenty other major character flaws. All that time they were growing, unchecked, in my personality while I concentrated on working on just one thing—my temper. I've inventoried the havoc I've caused during my life, and it turns out "temper problem" is way too understated to describe the mess that is me.

Sanctification? Yes, I no longer have the arrogant ignorance to believe that I'm always right, and I'm too embarrassed by the general sucktitude of my life to mount an angry fit every time something doesn't go my way. Getting better? I'm getting better at knowing what a wretched wreck I amount to, and it has shut me up and sat me down.

I don't know why no one believes this passage of Scripture, but I love it.

> But we have this treasure in jars of clay, to show that the surpass-
> ing power belongs to God and not to us. We are afflicted in every
> way, but not crushed; perplexed, but not driven to despair; perse-
> cuted, but not forsaken; struck down, but not destroyed; always
> carrying in the body the death of Jesus, so that the life of Jesus
> may also be manifested in our bodies. For we who live are always
> being given over to death for Jesus' sake, so that the life of Jesus
> also may be manifested in our mortal flesh.[3]

Let me attempt a snappier, more "victorious" retelling of the wisdom expressed in 2 Corinthians. I submit this revision as being much more in line with the Christianity of our time.

> But we have this treasure in saved, healed, delivered, and super-
> naturally changed vessels, to show that God has given to us, right
> now, his surpassing power over every situation. We are no longer
> afflicted, perplexed, in conflict, or defeated. No, we are alive with
> the power of Jesus, and the resurrection power of Jesus has

changed us now...*today!* And in every way! God wants you to see how impressive a Jesus-controlled person can be. When we strut our stuff in front of the unsaved, the power of Jesus is on display. And it becomes even more obvious that those who don't have this life are miserable and dying.

Contextual concerns aside, let's read Paul's words as a basic reality board to the Christian life: we're dying. Life is full of pain and perplexity. We have Christ, and so in the future his life will show up in us in resurrection and glory. In the present, that life appears in us in this very odd, contradictory experience. We are dying, afflicted, broken, hurting, confused...yet we hold on to Jesus in all these things and continue to love him and believe in him. The power of God is in us, not in sparing us from common human suffering and never giving us a free ride, but allowing us to be merely human yet part of a new creation in Jesus.

What does this mean?

It means your depression isn't fixed. It means you still want to look at pornography. It means you are still afraid of dying, find it difficult to tell the truth, and are purposely evasive when it comes to taking responsibility for your words and actions. It means you can lie, cheat, steal, deceive, and harm others when you are "in the flesh," which in one sense you always are. Even if you are a Christian, it means you are frequently miserable. And it means you are involved in a fight with your base nature over whether you will allow Christ to have more influence in your life. You want Jesus to overcome your broken, screwed-up, messed-up humanity. In fact, the greatest miracle is that with all the messes in your life, you still want to have Jesus as King.

But he said to me, "My grace is sufficient for you, for my power is made perfect in weakness." Therefore I will boast all the more gladly of my weaknesses, so that the power of Christ may rest upon me. For the sake of Christ, then, I am content with weaknesses, insults, hardships, persecutions, and calamities. For when I am weak, then I am strong.[4]

This language from 2 Corinthians is even more undeniable and unarguable. Weaknesses are with us through the entire journey. Paul was particularly thinking of persecution, but how much more does this passage apply to human frailty and hurt? How essential is it for us to be broken if Christ is going to be our strength? When I am weak, I am strong. Not "when I am cured" or "when I am successful" or "when I am a good Christian," but "when I am weak." The human experience of weakness is God's blueprint for calling attention to the supremacy of his Son. When miserably failing people continue to belong to, believe in, and worship Jesus, God is happy.

SO WHEN CAN WE START SINNING?

A number of readers are getting nervous, fearing that I'm about to tell everyone to go sin themselves up and forget about sanctification. That's not me. The conflict between human brokenness and sanctification is one of semantics. Or perhaps a better way to say it is "imagination." How do we imagine the life of faith? What does living faith look like? Does it look like a good Christian, a whole person, a victorious life? Which version of active sanctification does the life of faith reflect?

Faith, alive in our weakness, looks like a war. It's an impossible war waged against an untiring adversary: our sinful, fallen nature. Faith fights this battle. Author and pastor John Piper comes back often to Romans 8:13. I love this verse, and I need to explain why. If you're not careful, you can read it and conclude it sells the victorious life in the form of winning at life.

Romans 8:13 says: "For if you live according to the flesh you will die, but if by the Spirit you put [are putting] to death the deeds of the body, you will live."

The complexity resides right here: Faith is a lack of contentment with what I am, but a sense of satisfaction with what God has given me of himself in Jesus. The mark of saving faith is not just resting passively in the promises of the gospel (though that is exactly what justification does), but it's an ongoing war with the reality of my condition. My fight is never finished, because my sinful, messed-up human experience isn't finished until I die and am resurrected to live in a new world. The ongoing war between my old nature, which resists God, and my new nature, given to me by God and designed to draw me to him, is the normal life of a believer.

The life of faith is warfare. I fight. Jesus will finish the work. I will groan and do battle, climbing the mountain of holiness bearing wounds and battle scars. But I will climb it, since Christ is in me. The gospel assures victory, eventually.

What does this fight look like? It's a bloody mess. There is a lot of failure in it. It is a battle where we are brought down again and again. Brought down by what we are and what we continually discover ourselves to be. And we are victorious only in the victory of Jesus, a victory that is ours by faith, but not one we will fully enjoy until its conclusion.

I fall down. I get up…and believe. Over and over again. That's as good as it gets in this world. The life of faith is a battle fought in weakness and brokenness. The only soldiers are wounded ones.

For too long Christians have been presenting the gospel as a solution to trouble, when in fact it's a lifelong battle against one's own sin. If anything, it's a life that is far more uncomfortable than one's life before encountering Christ. Back then, we could simply live at will, without thoughts of God and his claim on our lives. Even after we get a new heart and a new life through God's grace, the sin we are killing in sanctification still resides in each one of us. It's not some demon or serpent external to us. Our battle is with our proclivities and preferences, our natural bent. Reaching the place where we embrace this fact is the foundation of the gospel's power in our lives.

The denial of the reality of the ongoing spiritual battle lands people in churches where they are turned into a cheering section for personal victory. They have enthusiasm, but they are cheering for a lie. The battle rages and it does not end until Jesus ends it. Those who claim victory prematurely may be describing their experience at the moment, but it doesn't describe the whole person, the whole story, or the reality of a Christian's life. They are still a mess. Count on it. This battle and the victories in it are fought by unvictorious Christians.

In every moment when I am winning, Jesus is with me. And in every moment when I am losing, Jesus is with me. At any moment when I am confused, wounded, and despairing, Jesus is with me. I never, ever, lose the brokenness. I fight and sometimes I prevail, but I can't prevent more of my screwed-up, messed-up life from erupting. Because I belong to One whose resurrection guarantees that I will arrive safely home in a new body and be part of a new creation, I miraculously, amazingly, find myself continuing to believe, continuing to move forward, until Jesus picks me up and takes me home.

COMMON CHRISTIAN LIES ABOUT GOD

Now we come to something very important. The constant emphasis on the victorious life or the good Christian life is the Antichrist as it pertains to the gospel. Here's why. If I am _____ (fill in your favorite victorious-life terminology), then will I be in a position to be grateful for what Jesus did when he was executed on the cross? Perhaps at first I will be overwhelmed with gratitude toward Christ. But over time, as I find that I'm capable of maintaining victory in my life, I will need Jesus less and less. I still want him to meet me at the gate on the way into heaven, but right now I'm doing great without him. I'm a good Christian.

If you embrace this take on the Christian journey, it will kill you.

We need our brokenness. We need to admit it and know it is the real, true stuff of our earthly journey in a fallen world. It's the cross on which

Jesus meets us. It is the incarnation he takes up for us. It's what his hands touch when he holds us.

In his book *Mortal Lessons,* physician Richard Selzer describes a scene in a hospital room after he had performed surgery on a young woman's face:

> I stand by the bed where a young woman lies, her face postoperative, her mouth twisted in palsy, clownish. A tiny twig of the facial nerve, the one to the muscles of her mouth, has been severed. She will be thus from now on. The surgeon had followed with religious fervor the curve of her flesh; I promise you that. Nevertheless, to remove the tumor in her cheek, I had cut the little nerve.
>
> Her young husband is in the room. He stands on the opposite side of the bed, and together they seem to dwell in the evening lamplight, isolated from me, private. Who are they, I ask myself, he and this wry-mouth I have made, who gaze at and touch each other so generously, greedily? The young woman speaks.
>
> "Will my mouth always be like this?" she asks.
>
> "Yes," I say, "it will. It is because the nerve was cut."
>
> She nods, and is silent. But the young man smiles.
>
> "I like it," he says. "It is kind of cute."
>
> All at once I *know* who he is. I understand, and I lower my gaze. One is not bold in an encounter with a god. Unmindful, he bends to kiss her crooked mouth, and I so close I can see how he twists his own lips to accommodate to hers, to show her that their kiss still works.[5]

This is who Jesus has always been. And if you think you are getting to be a great kisser or are looking desirable, I feel sorry for you. He wraps himself around our hurts, our brokenness, and our ugly, ever-present sin.

Those of you who want to draw big, dark lines to separate your humanity and your sin, go right ahead. But I won't be joining you.

My humanity, my sin, it's all me. And I need Jesus to love me like I really am: brokenness, wounds, sins, addictions, lies, death, fear…all of it. Take all of it, Lord Jesus. If I don't present this broken, messed-up person to Jesus, my faith is dishonest, and my understanding of faith will become a way of continuing the ruse and pretense of being good.

I understand that Christians need—desperately—to hear experiential testimonies of the power of the gospel. I understand as well that it's not pleasant to hear that we are broken and are going to stay that way. I know there will be little enthusiasm for saying sanctification consists, in large measure, in seeing our sin and acknowledging how deeply and extensively it has marred us. No triumphalist will agree that the fight of faith is not a victory party but a bloody war on a battlefield that resembles Omaha Beach.

But that's the way it is. I'm right on this one.

I frequently hear of well-known Christians, even leaders, who are depressed. Where do they turn for help? How do they admit their hurt? It seems so unchristian to admit being depressed, yet it is a reality for millions of people. Porn addiction. Food addiction. Rage addiction. An obsessive need to control others. Chronic lying and dishonesty. How many pastors and Christian leaders live with these human frailties and never seek help because they can't admit what we all know is true about all of us? They preach about salvation, love, and Jesus, but inside they feel like the damned.

Multiply this by the hundreds of millions of broken Christians. They are merely human, but their church says they must be better than human to be good Christians. They aren't allowed to acknowledge their troubled lives. Their marriages are wounded. Their children are hurting. They are filled with fear and the sins of the flesh. They are depressed and addicted, yet they can approach the church only with the lie that all is well. If it somehow becomes apparent that all is not well, they avoid the church. They already feel sufficiently condemned without showing up on Sunday to receive even more condemnation.

I don't place the entire blame on the church. We all prefer to avoid the mirror. So even if a church encourages transparency and doesn't judge those who are candid about their struggles, there are many who still opt for secrecy. But with so few churches and individual Christians telling the truth about their brokenness, I blame all of us who know better. We know the victorious Christian life is not the message of Jesus, but we are afraid to live otherwise. What if someone found out we're not a good Christian?

I close with something I have said many times before. The prodigal son, there on his knees with his father's touch upon him, was not a victorious Christian. He was broken, a failure. And even in his desperate return home, he wasn't being honest. He wanted religion more than grace. He wanted a meal and a place to live, even if it was among the servants. At least it would be more food and better lodging than he had been getting. But instead of being given religion, the son was baptized in mercy and resurrected in grace. His brokenness was wrapped up in the robe and the embrace of God.

Why do we pretend that we are better than that boy? Why do we make the resentful, self-righteous older brother the goal of Christian experience? Why do we want to add an epilogue to the parable, where the younger brother straightens out and becomes a successful youth speaker, writing books and touring the country doing youth revivals?

Lutheran writer Hermann Sasse, in a meditation on Martin Luther's last words, "We are beggars. This is true," puts it perfectly:

> Luther asserted the very opposite: "Christ dwells only with sinners." For the sinner and for the sinner alone is His table set. There we receive His true body and His true blood "for the forgiveness of sins" and this holds true even if forgiveness

has already been received in Absolution. [The fact] that here Scripture is completely on the side of Luther needs no further demonstration. Every page of the New Testament is indeed testimony of the Christ whose proper office it is "to save sinners," "to seek and to save the lost." And the entire saving work of Jesus, from the days when He was in Galilee and, to the amazement and alarm of the Pharisees, ate with tax collectors and sinners; to the moment when he, in contradiction with the principles of every rational morality, promised paradise to the thief on the cross, yes, His entire life on earth, from the cradle to the Cross, is one, unique grand demonstration of a wonder beyond all reason: The miracle of divine forgiveness, of the justification of the sinner. "Christ dwells only in sinners."[6]

13

Leaving Behind
the Church-Shaped Life

Life as a Jesus-follower grows out of Jesus and the gospel, not out of the church. The church is a resource for spiritual development and can be a sign of what God wants to do on earth. But the church, because it is neither Christ nor his Kingdom, is never the ultimate source of a person's life with God.

The life of grace is watered, nurtured, and encouraged by the church when it is following Christ and committed to being a movement Jesus would recognize as his own. When the church is off track, however, it's a massive discouragement to many who want to follow Jesus. Understanding the difference between the church-shaped life and what Jesus was creating in his disciples is vital if you want to experience Jesus-shaped spirituality.

If you have left a church or are considering doing so, you have no doubt heard churchgoing Christians say you can't live the Christian life or be a disciple if you are not "in" a church. The claims may have stung or made you angry, or aroused leftover guilt from childhood, or made you feel judged or lied to. Or perhaps you found yourself agreeing with them and simply stopped calling yourself a Christian.

SANDLOT BASEBALL AND THE MAJOR LEAGUES

Let's consider an illustration of the relationship between the life of faith and the churches that nurture and promote it. Anyone who knows me will tell you I am a devoted fan of baseball. I follow the Cincinnati Reds, but I am, in reality, a fan of the game itself. I love baseball at every level. I love the history of the game, the aesthetics, the drama, and the contribution to civic life. There's not any form of the game of baseball that I don't enjoy.

At least part of that love grows out of a wonderful childhood memory. In the center of our neighborhood were two large vacant lots, separated by an alley and perfect for every game known to the world of kids, but especially baseball. From the time I was old enough to leave my yard, I have memories of ball games in what we called "the field." I can still walk you through the bases (second base was a tree) and still experience the feeling of a ball dropping out of the heavens toward my position in right field, despite all my prayers asking that it would never happen.

We took baseball seriously. We played by the rules, or at least as best as we could at our age. We let new kids in with minimal hazing. We had a great time imagining that we were real baseball players. We were, of course, just kids, and no one was expecting us to be professionals. Umpires were optional, but that didn't mean we wouldn't argue the game passionately or that we didn't care about baseball.

A few blocks away were several community ballparks. Little League and Babe Ruth League. High school and American Legion ball. Coaches. Uniforms. Lights. Announcers. Real umps. Real cleats. Parents. The occasional newspaper photographer. For us, that was the big leagues. That was real baseball, not just the kids' game going on over at the field. There was, however, an important connection between the game played on the field, the game played at the local ballpark, and even the major-league game of the week on television.

The wise men of baseball have always understood that connection. The best players at every level know that the game of baseball didn't begin as the national pastime or an organized set of leagues (National and American) with an all-star break, the play-offs, and the World Series. The game

exists first and foremost in the imagination and exuberance of kids playing ball at "the field." And only because it exists in the lives of kids can it
exist anywhere else.

Baseball grew out of the devotion and joy kids had for the game.
It existed in the experience and memory of children, young people,
and amateurs before it existed as an organized, professional sport. The
development of baseball as an institution—made up of leagues, team
franchises, the Hall of Fame, rules, and umpires—rests on this fragile
foundation: the pleasure and experience that young people find in
playing ball.

As Major League Baseball has learned with some of its controversies—
the strike and cancellation of the World Series, the ongoing steroid scandal, records with an asterisk added—if the kids start deciding to play
soccer down at "the field," it won't be long before baseball is in trouble.
It's no accident that every baseball franchise (and Major League Baseball
in general) is busy promoting baseball at the local level in boys' and girls'
clubs, park districts, and school yards. They understand the connection
between their game and the pleasures of the kids' game.

If the institutional side of baseball ever forgets this, there will be dis-
aster. Much like what happens when the church begins to believe that
the lives of disciples grow inside its walls, through its programs, and
guided by its organizational playbook, rather than in the lives of individual believers who are drawn to Jesus.

The Holy Spirit transforms individuals into Jesus-followers, but Jesus
was explicit about the purpose of the church, which is to make disciples.
Does that mean the church replaces the Holy Spirit? No, it means the
church is a community that the Holy Spirit uses to bring individuals to
mature Christlikeness and genuine Kingdom usefulness. The balance between an individual's faith, Jesus Christ, and the Holy Spirit is vital and
delicate. Once lost or distorted, it must be corrected, or a counterfeit
Christian existence will grow in place of the real thing.

A CLOSE LOOK AT THE CHURCH-BASED LIFE

If you have left the church but still want to follow Jesus, how should you evaluate your past church experience and the influence the church had on your life? What is to be learned from the Christian experience that grows out of church-based discipleship?

Perhaps nothing is more representative of church-shaped Christianity than the idea of a discipleship course or the task of learning discipleship principles through a weekly class. Let me be very clear that I am in no way opposed to such courses or their content, but pause for a moment to consider the format and structure. And as you do, think about how Jesus taught discipleship.

First, Jesus made disciples through relationship and as a result of observation. The disciples—who were a bunch of blue-collar, nonrabbinical types—weren't taking notes or memorizing Scripture, as important as the Scriptures are in spiritual formation. Instead, they were observing Jesus, their Mentor and Friend. They heard his words repeatedly, but they primarily observed his actions, routines, reactions, and interactions. This is why the Gospels are so full of Jesus' actions, miracles, and journeys. His disciples—both then and now—were to learn from his life as a living curriculum. Living in that relationship and observing it from every angle was the basic stuff of living and learning.

Second, Jesus made disciples out of these followers through their constant exposure to his teachings. The most complete curriculum for disciples are the words, parables, sermons, prophecies, and teachings of Jesus. Again, the four Gospels reflect this, with the obvious intention that Christians would have the words and teachings of Jesus preserved as the core content of discipleship.

Third, Jesus put his disciples in a variety of situations that took them far beyond their comfort zones. This included preaching tours, visiting Gentile areas, going to Samaria (land of the despised, mongrelized descendants of Babylonians and Assyrians), interacting with outcasts, and confronting religious leaders. It's certain that Jesus did this so that his disciples would experience the gospel of the Kingdom in the same contexts that his followers would face in the future. As they went into these situations, they were deeply impressed with the relevance and power of the message and power of Jesus for all kinds of people.

Fourth, Jesus allowed his followers to experience the power of the Holy Spirit for themselves. Sometimes this was in ministry leadership, at other times it was through miracles, suffering, or even failure. The disciples were sometimes overwhelmed by the power of the Spirit, but they did not miss the lesson: What was happening with Jesus would continue beyond Jesus' years on earth. There always would be a demonstration of the power of God's Spirit in the world.

Fifth, it's clear that, for Jesus, participation in institutional Judaism—the church of his day—did not equal discipleship or participation in the movement he was creating. In fact, Jesus frequently contrasted not just the religion of the Pharisees but Judaism itself with his own movement. He said that his movement could not be contained in the "old wineskins" of Judaism, but was "new wine" that demanded new wineskins.[1] Given what we know of Jesus' work and teachings to establish the Kingdom of God, there is no way to present Jesus as establishing an institutional religion restricted to names on a membership roll or people present in a building.

The movement Jesus started was the fulfillment and completion of the old covenant. With Jesus' bringing his Kingdom on earth, the law could be written on the heart, not stored away on stone tablets. Now the Spirit of God would come to every believer, not just to a few. Now a new circumcision was proclaimed in baptism. Now the people of God included those from every tribe, nation, and language. Now there would be no earthly temple, priest, or king. As all these were fulfilled, Jesus' movement would not be found in these forms again but in himself and through the work of God's Spirit.

Sixth, Jesus created disciples by the power of the Holy Spirit illuminating the gospel in retrospect. The gospel of John tells us that the apostles, after witnessing the events and hearing the teachings of Jesus' ministry, often realized the meaning later with the aid of the Holy Spirit. Even during Jesus' post-resurrection appearances to his followers, the Spirit was illuminating the presence of Christ in the world and in the Scriptures.

It's obvious to see that the Holy Spirit is the essential power of Jesus' movement. The Spirit is like the wind. He goes into the human heart to do what no human being can do for another human being. This is the Spirit who leads, equips, befriends, teaches, counsels, convicts, and glorifies.

At no point does Jesus place the Holy Spirit under the control of human leadership or suggest that the Spirit will be dispensed exclusively by human means. In the book of Acts, we read that the church in Jerusalem waited on the Spirit and prayed for the Spirit, but Revelation chapters 2 and 3 make it obvious that church congregations can exist without the power of the Holy Spirit. A church claiming to have the Holy Spirit and the authority of Jesus is not to be believed without genuine evidence.

Seventh, Jesus created disciples who were called and centered in the gospel announcement of what God was doing at the time. They were not called to relive the past or to preserve old forms and practices. Whatever Jesus did in his process of making disciples, the end result is plain. He formed a community of disciples from every nation, obeying what Jesus taught, participating in the announcement of God's victorious reign, and demonstrating the power of the Holy Spirit. Disciples are witnesses to the world until the Kingdom arrives in full.

GOD'S KINGDOM, NOT YOUR FAVORITE CHURCH

Have you ever met Christians who, when asked what it means to be a Christian, begin talking about their church? I'm happy for anyone who has a great church experience, but being associated with a church does not define what it means to be a Christian.

Jesus wanted the life of his disciples to grow out of Kingdom-of-God soil. That Kingdom takes root in the lives of disciples who were changed by the gospel. While signing up to take a discipleship class can give believers a plan for reading the Bible and many helpful ideas on prayer, your relationship with God grows uniquely in the soil that is your journey through life. Jesus meets you at places that are meaningful to you; he speaks to you as an individual, and he grows his influence in you in unique ways. You aren't defined by anyone else's map of the Christian life, even if those maps might be helpful in some ways.

Yes, every Christian needs to know a shared core of essential Christian teaching. But for many churches, "discipleship" means taking every Jesus-follower and turning him or her into a cloned product of that church's program, goals, and agenda. If those include taking the gospel into the world, making disciples, and doing the works of Jesus as Jesus did, then such a church will provide a useful and helpful home base for the life of faith. However, if being a Christian becomes a club membership with an outsourced mission and applause for the people on the big screen, that is not an environment for becoming Jesus-shaped, no matter how big the crowd.

Following Jesus is more than core information and an institutional job description. It is about where God has placed you. It is about your relationships, your gifts (and not just those the church can use in its programs), your stewardship of possessions, and your particular map of Kingdom territory. You have a mission from your King. The church is called to serve and resource you as you live the Jesus-filled life in the world.

As I type this, I'm glancing at the weekly newsletter from one of my favorite churches. The leadership is dedicated to equipping every Christian in that church family to spend his or her life as an agent of the Kingdom wherever they live and work. The leadership preaches and teaches the Jesus message. They present opportunities to practice the disciplines of discipleship. This church's primary goal is to support every disciple in his or her mission in the world, not to draw them into the church's programs five nights a week.

One of the saddest realities I've experienced is the large number of people who have no concept of discipleship apart from what their church and its programs offer. Their concept of the Christian life is no more Kingdom oriented or Spirit filled than a meeting of the local women's club or a Thursday-night bowling league. This is sad, because we are called to live as disciples of Jesus as we relate to others in service clubs, bowling leagues, skateboard parks, pubs, classrooms, with the homeless, in women's shelters, in twelve-step groups, in the arts, among the dying, and so on. We live in a vast and diverse world. It's not a world where God has restricted the practice of Christian faith to the church calendar.

Listen, my "leaving" brother or sister: God hasn't kicked you out of anything. He has sent you into his world. You may be the one person who can bring the Kingdom to the world you inhabit every day. You might represent the one relationship that touches the overlooked and left-out person. Rather than think about quitting and leaving, why not think about what it means to be sent?

Abraham was told by God, Leave…and I'll show you what you need to see along the way.[2]

Jonah ran away from God and God's people as fast and as far as he could. Why was Jonah—the whiny, disobedient prophet—the one messenger God wanted to send to the Assyrian capital to announce God's judgment and mercy? God could have sent anyone to Nineveh, but he handpicked Jonah.

Moses left Egypt and God worked with him for forty years, turning Moses into a unique multicultural leader for the deliverance of his people.[3]

Joseph was rejected repeatedly, all in a design to bring him to the place where he could rise to power and ensure the survival of his family.[4]

How often did Jesus say we would have to leave security and comfort to follow him?[5] He said it again and again, so why is it so easy for Christians to overlook his clear teaching?

Much of what passes for proclaiming Jesus is, in actuality, churches concerned with attracting large numbers on Sunday mornings, directing financial resources toward church budgets, and showing Christians how to get in synch with church activities. What's needed is a wave of churches that are committed to helping you become a missionary in your world.

NOT LEAVING, BUT BEING SENT

Millions of Christians have moved out of the traditional church and into the culture. They have moved into alternative forms of the church and into new and little-understood expressions of the church. What are these Christians looking for, and what are they finding? I believe they want to affirm a balance of Jesus, Kingdom of God, church, and individual life.

There have been times in my church-dominated, church-shaped experience when I caught the sound and sight of something entirely different from what I was experiencing. I'm not talking about the plastic happiness of pretend spirituality, nor am I talking about impressive rooms full of rocking-out worshipers.

When I caught sight of something that was so different and real that it captured my attention and drew my spirit, it was always a person. It was the appeal of a person who chose the way of Jesus and not the way of money, success, popularity, or fame. They were not looking for a bigger crowd. They were not looking to sell books or make their name famous. They did not show up to attract an audience or attention. They showed up to give to others.

They gave away their money and chose suffering. They were little known or unknown but lived openly and honestly before God.

They saw the possibility of God's Kingdom in places such as senior-adult apartment complexes, AIDS hospices, Alzheimer's wards, mountain schools, and remote villages far from their home.

They never pointed to anything as much as Christ, the gospel, and the love of Jesus.

Their beliefs and actions flowed together seamlessly. Love, faith, hope, and good works were inseparable.

They were humble, silent when necessary, and speaking up as the Holy Spirit led. The great expression of their faith was to serve in Jesus' name and to count all things valuable only in relationship to Christ.

The humble servants of Jesus, the believers who serve Christ and his Kingdom asking for nothing, remind me that the beauty of the life of discipleship is "He must increase, but I must decrease."[6] This life grows in the soil of Jesus' life, death, and resurrection. It is the church's calling to produce disciples who hunger for Jesus, and it is the believer's calling to know the difference between Jesus and the church that points to Jesus.

Wisdom knows the narrow path is seldom crowded. Imagine what the critics and the defenders of the status quo said about Abraham when he left a wealthy, comfortable life in Ur. Imagine what those on the sidelines said about the original disciples, who left jobs and families to follow an iconoclastic rabbi. Imagine what church leaders said about Martin Luther, St. Francis, Menno Simons, William Tyndale, John Wesley, William Booth, and many, many others.

Now we move on to more critical questions: What kind of life do you want as a Christian? What are the longings of your heart that you carry with you, no matter where you find yourself?

14

Jesus, Honesty, and the Man Who Wouldn't Smile

I love outbursts of honesty.

If you are a typical adult, you live most of your life in a world of carefully contrived presentations and controlled expressions. You say hundreds of things you don't mean, and you understand that others do the same. "How are things?" "Great! How about you?" "Oh, I can't complain. Hey, let's get together some time." "Sure, that would be great."

For years I've complimented every baby I see, insisting they are cute. To tell the truth, I've lied on more than one occasion. But who wants all that trouble?

"Do I look fat in this dress?" There is only one answer there, dude. Your dedication to honesty will not pay off when replying to that question. And when the teacher says, "Your kids are amazing," entertain the possibility that you might not be the only parent who hears that line during Meet the Teacher night.

Social conventions, corporate culture, and the customs of casual human relationships all require that we sacrifice a good deal of honesty. We're expected to smile, nod, and utter glib and meaningless comments every day. If you choose to undermine this social contract, you will stand out, and you'll pay the price for doing so. From Jesus to Martin Luther King Jr. to artists such as Woody Guthrie and Derek Webb, honesty that gives the lie to the conspiracy of pretense is a risky ride.

This might explain the appeal that religion still holds for so many people. Religion provides a blanket of insulation for those who are happy to go along with the superficial social conventions. Religion tells us how to act and what to say at life's difficult moments. Religion often provides a script of polite, stoic, pious, and acceptable behavior to insert into moments of great questioning, pain, and disappointment. You don't know what to say? Just read the card, and we'll all get through this skit called life.

Most religious institutions are expert at producing this kind of social spirituality. Once you are told what it means to be a good Christian, you know how you're expected to react. You know how you should express yourself and what constitutes a good witness—even when your own life is falling apart. These expectations can extend to a dress code, acceptable facial expressions, the recommended tone of voice, appropriate physical gestures, and, of course, preapproved statements and sentiments.

FINDING AN HONEST HERO

I have an odd collection of spiritual heroes, one of whom is the singer-songwriter Mark Heard. Heard holds an important place in the history of my faith, and it's because he stopped smiling. When he released his first album on a Christian record label, his face was grinning all over the cover. I wouldn't blame anyone for doing the same. He was happy to have an album coming out after years of writing and playing music; so why not smile?

It became apparent on subsequent albums, however, that Heard wasn't your typical Christian artist. His lyrics were sensitive and deeply poetic. They seldom mentioned Jesus in the expected way. They explored a great variety of human experiences and emotions. You never knew what he was going to say next, and in Christian music that just isn't done.

Over time he took complete control of his music. He became one of the first contemporary Christian musical artists to make music that took risks by breaking the usual formulas and sought something other than mainstream acceptance. Dozens of significant songwriters and performers, such as Bruce Cockburn and Pierce Pettis, pay respect to Mark Heard as an influence.

Along the way, he almost completely stopped smiling in his photographs. On his albums and in personal photos, he never grinned like a hallelujah revival singer. He looked somber, sometimes sad. Unlike the standard, happy-clappy grins of other Christian musicians, Heard's image said, "I'm not playing the game. I'm human like you, and my faith doesn't make me grin all the time. I'm not a clown. I hurt. I have real questions and struggles. Jesus isn't a way to get high or to make everything easy."

Heard died young, but his artistic integrity and personal honesty were like water in the desert. Many believers like me were lost in the clownish happiness and manufactured spirituality of the evangelical wilderness, yearning for a flag that signaled there was another way to live. For me, Mark Heard was waving the flag of spiritual honesty.

I'm not a recording artist, but I have emulated Heard in one way: I refuse to be a grinning Christian. Last year a temporary employee showed up in our town's post office as a summer replacement for the postmaster. I saw her every morning for a couple of weeks, and then she asked me, "Are you a preacher?" That really wasn't a piece of ace detective work, considering the usual stream of mail that landed in my box from religious sources and addressed to Rev. Spencer. So I assured her that I was, to which she said, with a bit of alarm, "Then you need to smile a lot more!"

Around our house I've had a lot of fun with that story. But it makes me wonder to what extent we've bought into a prefabricated religious ideal that obliterates the reality of life as a Christian. How many people are convinced they are following Jesus because they are faithfully following a script they were handed? And some are even willing to call you out at the post office if you dare go off script.

A couple of times in my journey, I've gone way off the map that my fellow Baptists have been reading. Sometimes it's in what I write. I've been too honest, according to their view, in spite of the model we find in the Psalms, the prophets, St. Paul, and Jesus. Sometimes I get in trouble for my public speaking. I'm not safe enough or predictable enough. Most sermons conform so closely to the established pattern and are delivered in such a predictable, rote format that veteran churchgoers know the end once they've heard the first three minutes. Meanwhile, newcomers are singsonged to sleep by the staleness of it all.

Sometimes when I've gone off script, I've been called aside and told, "You can't say that."

"Really? Why?"

"Well, that's not what Christians are supposed to say."

"So you know in advance what Christians are supposed to say, how they are supposed to act, what they are supposed to feel? Where did you get this information?"

I have yet to find a critic who has a good answer to that question. They can't answer because the sanctioned Christian script they rely on didn't come from anyone resembling Jesus. Anything from him will be unpredictable and unsettling, honest and unexpected, because he was the most "off the map" Person who ever lived.

In the last lines of *King Lear*, one character looks at the tragic outcome of the story and says, "The weight of this sad time we must obey; Speak what we feel, not what we ought to say."[1]

Christians often are told to speak, feel, and act as they are supposed to, in order to avoid upsetting anyone. But with that kind of inoffensive, neutered, spray-tan spirituality loose in the Christian world, the small protests of Mark Heard, Anne Lamott, Robert Capon, Henri Nouwen, Dietrich Bonhoeffer, and Bono—communicators who have discarded the script and walked a more provocative path—become very important. The real life of faith, produced by the Holy Spirit, matters like water in a desert.

We need to pay attention to people who are unlikely Jesus-followers. We need to learn from Christians who walk on and away from the traditional pathways, as well as those who don't play the game by the usual rules. In pursuing Jesus-shaped spirituality, the heroes you identify are important.

I pay close attention to a gallery of honest saints: Johnny Cash, Rich Mullins, Thomas Merton, Sara Miles, Robert Capon, Martin Luther, Wendell Berry, Bono, Flannery O'Connor, Lottie Moon, Tony Campolo, St. Patrick, Bill Mallonee, Clarence Jordan, Martin Luther King Jr., John Wesley, Charles Spurgeon, J. C. Ryle, Mark Heard, T. S. Eliot, Barkley Moore, Michael Been, and Derek Webb. All are heroes of mine who remind me that Jesus-shaped spirituality rarely follows the printed program.

PURSUING AN UNSCRIPTED LIFE

The life of faith ought to be marked by walking in the light of honesty. It's particularly strange when we talk about the realities of sin, confession, repentance, and the cross but whitewash it all in favor of the nice face of socially accepted, domesticated religion.

I'm a large person, and like most large persons, I've done my share of things to try to motivate myself to lose weight. Several years ago when I was involved with starting a twelve-step ministry for alcoholics in my church, I decided to join Overeaters Anonymous. I got out the local directory, found a group that was meeting at a church I was familiar with, and headed off to a meeting. I am aware that OA is for people who struggle with all kinds of eating disorders, but it was odd when I arrived and discovered a room full of young, skinny, attractive women. There were no ugly men and no fat people at all.

For the next three weeks, I dutifully showed up, waiting for another fat guy to arrive and prove that I wasn't sitting in the wrong meeting. As I waited, I heard skinny women talk about not getting fat. I never heard a fat person say a word, because there was only one in the group—me. Not being a one-hundred-ten-pound, twenty-five-year-old single woman struggling to not eat chocolate cake, I didn't really feel included. I'd eaten the cake and all its relatives several times. In fact, I was getting hungry as I sat there listening to skinny women talk about not eating.

The only word spoken to me—I promise—during the entire three weeks was this: "There's a men's group at _____ church on Tuesday nights." Translation: "This isn't the OA group for fat men. Migrate please."

Please don't get the wrong idea. I'm not belittling anyone's struggles with food. I realize I may have been meeting with people who struggle with very serious, even life-threatening eating disorders. The problem was that this particular OA group's personality had become skinny women. It was no longer for ordinary, male, overweight people like me.

It was decision time. I could stick around and take the risk of being the unwanted fat guy in the group. If I chose that route, I knew I wouldn't find a sponsor, and the version of the twelve steps I was going to hear would be very different from my own story. My other choice was to take my problem and leave. Which I did. I couldn't say I was rejected, but I felt that I'd crossed into someone else's territory, and my presence would have been unwanted, even divisive.

Given that this book isn't about weight loss but about experiencing God, does anyone in the class want to make the connection? Yes, I see that hand.

Christians, no matter what their big struggles are, have a commonality in Jesus Christ and the gospel. We're all sinners saved by grace alone, through faith alone, by Christ alone. Our commonality invites us to be distinctively ourselves. Jesus creates a community with honest spirituality, with no reason to adopt a false persona to protect ourselves. We all fit in what Jesus offers us in the gospel. We are free to be real, honest, and vulnerable.

The problem arises with what churches and individual Christians do with Jesus' message. They soften its directness and dilute its force to make it conform to their own preferences. They make it more convenient and more comfortable, more in keeping with their idea of what is acceptable. They make it polite and nice, something that has a better chance of being accepted.

And as they do those things, they create a class system. The upper echelon is populated by Christians who agree to the rules and conform to the conventions. If you're on board with the right doctrines and hold a membership in the right denomination, you're accepted.

But if you are uncertain about too many doctrinal nuances, and you question the accepted practices, don't count on being invited to join the club. Too many expressions of Christian spirituality exclude those who don't share a particular view on the finer points of doctrine. They elevate the secondary issues to the status of core requirements and spend too much energy setting parameters for who looks like, acts like, and talks like a Christian. It's no surprise, then, that people leave the church over revered, yet nonessential, matters.

So, I wonder, do we have the honesty to say exactly what we are looking for in Jesus-shaped spirituality? Can we all share in an outburst of honesty? Can we get past the acceptable scripts and unposted rules and describe what we are longing to experience?

HOW HONEST CAN YOU BE?

Two years ago a commenter on my blog had one of those brilliant moments. In powerful simplicity, he wrote, "I don't care if I ever hear another sermon."

In a lot of churches, the head usher would tackle that guy, gag him, and lock him in the janitor's closet. But I understand exactly what he is saying. (By the way, remember this guy's line if you ever want to create trouble. It's a real hand grenade.)

He wasn't saying he's too good to need any more Bible teaching. He wasn't whining about being bored and needing something new and novel to tickle his ears. He was saying that the model of spirituality that dominated his corner of Christianity tended to rely on a sermon's forty-minute information dump as the primary means of spiritual growth. He was worn out by it. At the time he commented on my blog, he didn't care if he ever heard another sermon.

Of course, the church is full of Christians who know just what you and I need: a sermon, plus another sermon, followed by a third sermon. Add a daily quiet time. Season the required nourishment with "read the Bible through." That's evangelical spiritual formation in a nutshell. Oh, plus take an offering.

The church often sounds like a chorus of voices claiming that humans are big brains on legs and nothing more. It is thought that we need more information. More data. More facts and lectures. It's as though we are what we hear, read, and think. So open up your brain and get ready to absorb more truth.

Behind this is a very un-Jesus-shaped view of being human, and it needs to be called out. The Holy Spirit does not call us to become an overstuffed theological brain with a vocabulary that requires its own laptop. How many Christians need to be conversant in a technical version of religious terminology that can be decoded only by a committee of seminary professors?

Christians aren't searching for big words to memorize, but they are searching for the authentic humanness of the gospel. They seek a full and genuine human experience, normal human life as God created and re-created it. We need humanness made alive in the incarnation. We hunger for created, incarnated, redeemed, and resurrected, but real, humanity.

We long to be human beings, fully alive to who we are, to God, and to one another.

We long for beauty and for experiences of simple awe.

We long for relational and emotional connection. We long to know we are not alone, to love and be loved, to be heard and to hear our human family.

We long for worship that engages all our senses. We long for mystery, not explanation. We long for symbolism, not just exposition. We long for a recognition of what it means for God to be God and for each of us to be God's son or daughter. We do not long to be God or to be super-humans, but to be ourselves.

We long for Jesus to come to us in every way that life comes to us, and not just in a set of propositions.

We long for honesty about the brutal pain and disappointments of life, and we long to hear the voices of others who are experiencing that brokenness.

We are tired of the culture of untruth that Christians sometimes perpetuate in their fear that someone will know about the alcohol in the closet, the porn on the computer, the unbelieving child, the nagging doubts, the frightening medical diagnosis, and the desperate fears.

We long for a spirituality of stillness, contentment, and acceptance in the place of spiritual competition and wretched urgency. We have grown weary and sick of being challenged to do more and to be more committed, more surrendered, more holy under our own power.

We long for prayer that is not a means to accomplish things, bring miracles, generate power, or impress an audience. We long for the depths of spirituality, not the show of being spiritual.

We long to be loved, to be quietly accepted, to be told to lie down in green pastures, to stop the race, and to pray in silence. To be given a spirituality of dignity, not a spirituality that is a feature of this week's sermon series on how to have more and better sex, make more money, raise obedient kids, achieve great things, and otherwise turn Jesus into a means to lay hold of the American dream.

We long to understand the spirituality of those whose religion does not make them argumentative, vengeful, belligerent, or bigoted but makes them beautiful servants of peace. We long to know the Bible's message and then be free to live it ourselves, not in imitation of celebrity preachers or best-selling authors. We want to be lifted up, not beaten down. We hope for a simple spirituality, not an exciting, never-before-experienced high we get from attending a big razzle-dazzle event.

The man who posted a comment on my blog spoke the truth. Many of us are convinced we have already heard every sermon that's out there. We are familiar with the same one hundred moral exhortations, the same life lessons, and the same theological necessities. We all can list the typical spiritual demands, spoken by one hundred pastors attempting to sound just like their favorite superstar pastor. We are weary of the same one hundred convenient half-truths—the acceptable, agreed-upon untruths.

We have heard evangelicalism's prosperity promises and its prevarications and protests at least one hundred times. Those of us who started attending church at a young age and have kept at it over the years could preach the standard sermons as well as most of the persons in the pulpit. We've heard the same script delivered with different spins. It is overwhelmingly all the same, and it is not the life we want.

Church has done one thing that has helped us: we now feel the emptiness in our souls, and we have realized that we need to find the real gospel, the honest Savior, and the promised life of the Spirit.

We owe this to ourselves and our children. If we stay in institutional evangelicalism, our kids will be demoralized by the same script that left us hungry and thirsty. The gassed-up, energized church machine is launching itself into the future with all the arrogance it can muster, replete with every answer and all wisdom, increasingly learning nothing and seeing little wrong with its lack of resemblance to Jesus.

In a rare, self-aware moment, some churches will admit that a generation is largely missing on Sunday mornings. But then, true to form, the churches that have lost a generation will place the blame on those who are missing. The people who have left because they are seeking reality and an undiluted experience with Jesus are accused of being "carnal," "worldly," and "out of fellowship with the Lord." They are no longer good Christians.

Some of us will finally say good-bye to this insanity. We will discover other ways, other paths, other pilgrims and friends. We will be hearing something else…Someone else. And some of us will stay in the institutional church, hoping for change. But the ones who stay will listen differently to the same sermons and will no longer adhere to all the requirements.

We all—both the leavers and those who would like to leave—will have an outburst of honesty about the Christian life. In the next part of this book, I'm going to invite you to do something in the spirit of radical honesty: discover the Jesus-shaped life in a very different experience of community.

PART 4

THE JESUS COMMUNITY

Finding, or Starting, a Community of Encouragement

15

The Good and Bad of Being Alone

A few years into our marriage and before the kids came along, my wife, who was employed as a nurse, was scheduled to work the night shift on Thanksgiving Day. Before she had to leave for work, we went out to dinner at a restaurant instead of preparing turkey and dressing at home.

I'll never forget that particular Thanksgiving meal at the ironically named Banquet Table buffet. We were already feeling a bit depressed that we couldn't enjoy Thanksgiving with our families, but the restaurant itself was even more depressing. Many people had come there alone and were sitting alone. Alone on Thanksgiving Day.

Some of those faces will live in my memory for years to come. They seemed to be lined with pain and rejection. The people seemed to be alone because life had been so hard for them that it took away the gift of family and love—the two things other people were enjoying in their homes that very moment. Those lonely people seemed to eat with a particular contempt for the idea of setting aside a day to be thankful.

I was glad when our meal was over. Even with just the two of us there, I felt I was having a feast in front of a group of starving people.

Of course, most of us have times when we actually like to be alone. I'm sitting alone in a large reading room at a library as I'm writing these words, and I've been content to be here all morning. I am happy for time alone when I can focus on thinking and writing. My wife is doing one of her favorite things today. She's spending the day at a Catholic retreat, "alone" with God.

Time alone can be part of powerful spiritual transformation. My own conversion was significantly affected by a day I was required to spend completely alone as part of a vigil on a church youth retreat. Away from the usual distractions and other people, the presence of the Holy Spirit became very real to me. I was "alone" with God. My need for Christ came to the front of my life that day. If I had been with Christians instead of being alone, I don't know if I would be a Christian now.

I counsel anyone—no matter what their role in life—to value time alone and to use it positively for prayer, meditation, or simply being still in God's constant presence. What a gift that can be in times when you are questioning, needing strength or direction, hurting, or simply hungering for God.

There is something about being human that demands and benefits from being alone, but there is also an aspect to aloneness that we recognize as depriving us of one of the best things about being human: our relationships with other people. We are made for a balance between solitude and community.

The balance of solitude and relationships runs deeply through most people. We understand that a person who is constantly alone or always with others runs the risk of being thrown out of balance. And, of course, we need to ask what this has to do with Jesus-shaped spirituality?

FINDING COMMUNITY OUTSIDE THE ORGANIZED CHURCH

Many who have left the church, or who find themselves moving away from it, describe their church experience as a feeling of being alone and isolated. On the surface, this seems to be a weak and selfish excuse for leaving the church. How can anyone be alone in a congregation where, if it's like my church, you're forced to stand up and shake hands with other people every Sunday? How can you feel alone when the entire church calendar is made up of group events and social activities, from corporate worship to sports teams? Churches send endless versions of the message "we want you to be involved" to their congregations. In most churches—especially large churches—it's clear that good Christians are expected to immerse themselves in one long, continuous social occasion. Given all the opportunities and encouragement to get involved, isn't it hard to believe that a person could feel alone in church?

Even more amazing to those who are devoted to institutional Christianity, people who leave the church often report that they feel far more included and accepted among those who are far outside the church.

My friend Andrew Marin posted a series of video interviews on his Web site, LoveIsAnOrientation.com. He taped interviews conducted with spectators at the annual Chicago gay pride parade. On camera in one of the interviews was "Will," a young evangelical Christian and seminary student. He is happily married and was marching in the parade. Andrew asked Will why he'd joined the parade, and Will said he experienced far greater acceptance and friendship in the gay community he sought to minister to than he did with seminary or church friends.

Will is not alone, as many of you already know. Thousands of Christians feel more comfortable in the nonreligious and non-Christian relationships in their lives than in the Christian relationships. I know Christians who have discovered that everything from bars to bowling leagues to AA meetings generate more genuine friendships and unconditional acceptance than many of their experiences of Christian fellowship. Why is it that Christian relationships, which are supposed to be vitally important to spiritual growth, so often lag behind other types of relationships?

Internet Monk reader Andrea wrote me to say that her experience in church was one of feeling constant exclusion because of her struggle with symptoms of mental illness and the effects of medication she was taking. She understood that her struggle with depression made her feel isolated, but she never met anyone in church who openly shared about their own struggles.[1]

Beyond being made to feel alone, Andrea never met another believer who accepted her as being "normal" in Christ. Instead, she felt there was a constant effort to keep her out of the way lest her struggle and "oddity" become too visible to people the church wanted to reach.

Jill is a friend who often shares her experience as a single woman attending a traditional church. She frequently plays the piano and sings, receiving lots of affirmation for her contributions to the quality of public worship. But her heart's desire is for something very simple: someone to pray with her and for her. She would love it if someone asked her, in a nonthreatening, nonembarrassing way, what she'd like prayer for.

I've sat through hundreds of hours of church prayer meetings. You can request prayer for every kind of illness, right down to the gory details of Uncle Todd's infected toe. If, however, you were to say that you're struggling financially or your marriage wasn't going well, the "awkward" buzzer would go off. Or mention that you just found out your son is gay or your daughter is pregnant by her boyfriend, and you'll feel the "no love" express heading your way. A gay son, pregnant unmarried daughter, financial struggles, or marital strife belongs in the "unspoken request" file. You can raise your hand and indicate you need prayer, but we'd prefer that you not be specific…especially if it's anything about your real life.

Why would someone in a struggling marriage feel they would get more sympathy from members of their bowling league than from people in church? Why would a person struggling with mental illness feel like a freak in her church? Why would a single woman find that her simple need for prayer was more trouble to the members of her church than it was worth? Why would Christians shift uncomfortably in their seats and quickly change the subject when someone shares that their teenage daughter is pregnant?

WHEN IT'S NOT GOOD TO BE ALONE

For Christians, being alone can have paradoxical outcomes. It can put you in closer touch with God, as Jesus modeled in his own life. But in the context of the church, being left alone, excluded, or isolated can alienate you from other Christians and intensify your pain.

I have experienced that type of isolation. Two years ago my wife began a journey that took her into the Roman Catholic Church. It was, to say the least, a surprise to me and something I wasn't able to understand. Because we both had been in ministry in Southern Baptist churches, this was a difficult journey for us. But it's one that God's grace and kindness saw through to its completion. I've never seen my wife happier in her relationship with the God she knows through Jesus. We love each other and rejoice that we belong to Jesus and share communion in him, if not at the same table.

My journey to this place of acceptance and rejoicing was, however, a terrible and painful ordeal. I battled overwhelming anger and bitterness. After thirty years of attending church together, I was devastated that God would allow this to happen. For the first time in my life, I was deeply, seriously hurting, and I needed Christians to come around me and support me.

Instead, I discovered what it was like to feel alone and unacceptable. My Christian friends were Baptists, raised on a steady diet of anti-Catholicism. To them, the idea that anyone would convert to the Roman Church was unthinkable, especially one spouse in a ministry marriage. Reactions ranged from silence to "Why does she want to worship Mary?" and other examples of Protestant mythology regarding Catholicism.

At times my emotions would spill over, but almost no one ever asked me to talk about why. More than a few fellow Christians criticized my obvious struggle and found fault with my family for going through this experience. (And don't ask what the Christian blogosphere thought. Ugh.) Only a very few Christians took time to comfort me in a Christlike way during what was clearly a disorienting experience for me.

If ever I felt like I was languishing in the evangelical wilderness, this was the time. I was almost completely alone, with no one to talk to who could listen helpfully. Having to pay a pastoral counselor for help seemed like an admission of defeat, an open declaration that so much that I had always believed about the church was a lie. I had hoped for concern and help, but most of the Christians in my life had no way to even think about what I was going through. (My wife, by the way, was surrounded by constant support and many new friends on her journey into the Catholic Church.)

One afternoon I had finished teaching my last class and was getting ready to lock up my classroom. Keeping myself emotionally nailed down had occupied me for the entire school day, and now I was starting to crack. I knelt on the floor to pick up a book and couldn't bring myself to stand back up.

My friend Paul stepped into the room with a worried look on his face. With no agenda other than concern, he said, "You aren't doing well, are you?" I couldn't even say yes or no. I nodded and he understood. He assured me of his prayers and compassion. He let me know it was okay for me to be broken. It was a small, Jesus-shaped moment, a moment that stood in stark contrast to the distance and discomfort I'd sensed from almost every other Christian I knew.

It's that aloneness that pushes people who want to love God and follow Jesus to leave the institutional church. It's what I mean when I say that many who leave are simply trying to find a way to survive spiritually.

Many leave the church because their aloneness is never recognized by others, and others in the church never realize their own sin in isolating the people in their midst. So those who don't conform and thus fail to fit in, for whatever reason, are left alone to be alone. When a person who feels isolated inside the church encounters acceptance and gracious concern from those who make no pretense of following Christ, it's a welcome gift in a desert. And it's a damning indictment of the church.

To find that the church doesn't want to take the risk and meet you halfway is devastating. Who wouldn't consider finding a new home outside the community of faith, when past attempts to make a home in the church were at best ignored, and at worst actively discouraged?

SACRED INDIVIDUALITY

There is a second kind of aloneness that many who have left the church share. It is the chosen aloneness of solitude and finding one's own spiritual path. The New Testament tells us that Jesus spent large amounts of time alone. There is a bit of a comedy track in the background of the gospel of Mark as the crowds that follow Jesus expecting miracles constantly find ways to ruin his efforts to be alone. One of his trips, more than one hundred miles from his home in Galilee, was interrupted by a mother asking him to drive a demon out of her daughter. Like a modern celebrity who can't enjoy a quiet meal in public, Jesus often was seeking solitude when his fans and followers were clamoring at his heels.[2]

How important is solitude for the Jesus-shaped disciple? It's essential because Jesus-shaped discipleship doesn't always happen to groups, even if some of it does happen in groups.

Churches love to promote Christianity as primarily a group activity. Participate in enough classes, conferences, concerts, projects, and committees, and you can become a follower of Jesus Christ just like everyone else. I have heard that story, sold it, and told it most of my life. Now I'm done with it.

When I was eleven years old, our church brought in an evangelist who met with the young people by age groups. Each group was brought into a room where the evangelist delivered a personal sermon on hell geared for that age group. He then invited everyone to make the decision to "get saved." Our group gathered, was preached to, and received the invitation. Everyone went forward and shook the preacher's hand and got baptized at the next worship service.

Everyone except me. I stayed in my seat and became something of a legend among the Sunday school teachers for my obstinacy. I couldn't have used the right words at age eleven, but I knew what group manipulation and peer pressure were all about. I wanted no part of it. In that part of my life, I wanted to be alone. When I began my journey to Christ, it was my own experience and not the pull of a group experience.

I admire Jesus-shaped disciples whose boldness and compassion grow out of this place of solitude. I want to be one who values relationships and community, but who is not defined by them. I want to have the certainty, confidence, and contentment that come from knowing who I am in the eyes and heart of God, not just who I am in relation to people.

At the foundation of the Christian life, there is a kind of sacred individuality, a sort of holy aloneness that cries out to be left alone with God. This isn't all of the Christian life. It doesn't erase those parts of a Christian's experience that happen in the context of relationships, but this sacred solitude needs to be discovered, respected, and protected.

It is that place where we most irrefutably hear God tell us that he loves us, and we come to know that, no matter what other people may say about us or do to us, God will not abandon us. That holy solitude is the place where we find God's Spirit changing our affections and redirecting our identities. It is, for Jesus-followers, holy ground.

There are many who leave the church because they find they are confronted by an inexplicable hostility toward solitude and individuality. In a community that says "God loves you," many feel that the next line is "and he dislikes everything about you." I've been around evangelical Christians every day for more than thirty years. The fear of individuality is deeply engrained in the church, and it extracts a terrible cost on a person's identity.

Many of those who represent and promote organized Christianity expect you to conform in ways that Jesus never required. They have expectations of dress—and I don't mean only among fundamentalists. They have expectations of how you will talk and even what words you will use. They know what books you should read, what athletes you should admire, what political candidates and parties you should support, and exactly how you should feel about controversial social issues.

There are expectations for your education, your finances, and your parenting methods. They don't hesitate to use the word *Christian* as an adjective in front of any number of things they believe all Christians must agree on. When you deviate, it makes them uncomfortable. Deviate enough and you're in trouble. Keep deviating, you'll be tossed out.

Individualists who are bold enough to make their approach to life and faith known upset the church's status quo. People who have a distinct individual identity break the unspoken, agreed-upon group rules. The individualists ask the wrong questions. They don't buy into the accepted assumptions. In short, they don't do what they are supposed to do.

Let an individualist run loose in the church, exercising his or her freedom and influencing other Christians, and soon our kids will begin to get the wrong ideas. The life expectancy of the people Martin Luther King Jr. referred to as the "creatively maladjusted" isn't encouraging. We may all bear the unique fingerprints of the divine, but the church prefers that all the sheep look, act, and sound exactly alike.

In other words, we're glad to have you. Here, put on your uniform, and read your script.

For many Christians who just can't buy all the peripheral church requirements, leaving the church is a decision to abandon the cold blanket of conformity. They have discovered that the crowd can't make them a Christian, but the crowd can certainly define Christianity so glibly that it's easy to be swayed, join the crowd, and become a counterfeit simply by osmosis. If you don't walk away, you risk losing your integrity as a believer.

Jesus is the Model for faithfully following God no matter what the group advocates, teaches, legislates, or demands. He was the most distinctive Individual of all time, and he possesses the power to make us both like himself and fully, completely ourselves. In Jesus is the power of holy solitude and Jesus-shaped community, and it's toward that kind of balance that we want to move.

ALONE AND TOGETHER, BOTH

Jesus-shaped spirituality recognizes the reality and value of being alone as well as the importance of community. This recognition grows out of Jesus himself: a solitary Man of prayer, and the Messiah who called every kind of person to sit at his table and enter his Kingdom.

Church-shaped spirituality avoids any responsibility to lend comfort and support to a person in his or her individual pain, especially if it's the type of struggle that makes good Christians uncomfortable. Church-shaped spirituality often does not respond to the suffering of individuals unless that suffering fits within the church's definition of legitimate pain. So a church that will minister to a widow might have nothing to say to the girl who had an abortion, the addicted, or the mentally ill.

At the same time, church-shaped spirituality invalidates individual integrity and uniqueness, demanding that all comply with the group requirements. In place of authentic partnership in the faith, it invites us to passively attend events where we will be entertained and instructed. It tells us to believe that being part of the group is the same as being a disciple of Jesus.

Church-shaped spirituality may encourage a Christian to have a personal quiet time, but the spiritual path of solitude and individuality is seldom taken. Are church leaders fully committed to developing disciples who are capable of standing and ministering on their own? Not often, at least in my experience. Instead, it is tempting for organized Christianity to continue to create followers who are dependent on the church to dispense Christianity through programs and activities. It is rare to see disciples who are not dependent on other people, but who have healthy relationships built on their own spiritual maturity.

Jesus-shaped spirituality imitates Jesus' deep personal pursuit of God. It respects the pain, longing, and lamentation of the believer as the heart's cry to know and experience God in the real world. Jesus-shaped spirituality understands that while the church and the relationships found there may be important, they are by no means exclusive or, in many cases, primary in the life of a disciple. It understands why the demon-delivered man in the fifth chapter of Mark wanted to go with the community of disciples but was sent back to tell his family and friends what great things the Lord had done for him.[3]

Jesus-shaped spirituality understands that Jesus was balancing out discipleship and the church when he asked Peter, "Do you love me?" — a question only an individual can answer—and then instructed Peter to "feed my lambs," which is a call to service in community.[4]

Jesus-shaped spirituality understands why Paul says we are free, but we are to use our freedom carefully and wisely.[5]

For a disciple of Jesus, the life of faith involves both time alone and togetherness. Jesus calls us as individuals. The decision to follow him is an individual decision and commitment. But the life of a Jesus-follower involves both time spent in solitude with God and life in a community of faith. This is the balance we are seeking in Jesus-shaped spirituality. How do we understand God in the experience of aloneness and solitude? How do we experience community that nurtures and encourages discipleship but doesn't seek to replace it?

Some church-leavers have taken a necessary step—leaving the community they had grown dependent upon in unhealthy and unhelpful ways. Other church-leavers have taken a healthy step toward discovering how to participate in and create healthy relationships and communities that produce disciples who are able to live in the balance of solitude and community.

In seeking solitude and balancing healthy community, we discover the healthy spirituality of Jesus. We turn away from churchianity—a church-dependent religion—and begin a relationship with the great variety of Christian communities around us. We approach healthy Christian community as disciples who are open to relationships and ministry with others.

This is the reality and challenge of Jesus-shaped spirituality.

The Evangelical Sellout

My wife has written a number of Christmas and Holy Week plays. One of her most popular, *Dream of the Magi,* is the story of Christmas told from the point of view of the wise men. Being a somewhat magiesque-looking man, and knowing the playwright rather well, I've occasionally played one of the leading roles.

There's nothing more fun at Christmastime than dressing up like a wise man and entering into the story of the birth of Jesus. I enjoyed my part incredibly, but there was this one performance...

It was a Saturday night in a large church auditorium, and that night I paid for my failure to adequately prepare. I have a good memory, but longer speeches do require extra memory work. I was dressed for the part, wearing the makeup, surrounded by other actors...and making up a speech almost entirely from my imagination.

Ad libs are part of the acting business, but this wasn't just a line or two. I had no idea what I was saying, but I kept talking anyway...and talking...and talking. Like a rookie pilot who realizes he doesn't know how to land a plane, I circled the airport several times before I finally found a way to get to the next cue.

My fellow actors looked at me with increasing alarm as I floundered in a soliloquy that no one had ever heard before. I couldn't see my wife's face, but I didn't need to. "What is he doing? What's he saying? Where's he going?"

I really don't remember all that much about any other play I've been in, but I vividly recall those few moments—minutes? hours?—standing in front of the audience, making up a speech out of my head and hoping no one would notice I was sinking.

If you have left the church or are about to do so, this recollection may prompt a familiar feeling for you. You are in the cast. You're on stage. Your name is in the program. You're wearing the costume. You've been given the script. But you don't know your lines, and you're just making it up. It's scary and you're not having fun. If there's an exit, you're taking it.

WHY PEOPLE LEAVE

Why have so many people become church-leavers? Perhaps many of them don't know how to live a good Christian life, and they are tired of playing the part. They'd rather be true to themselves than continue to act like they've gotten it all together. So they've left the stage.

Christianity is a rather odd religion in many ways. It would be easier to be a Muslim. With Islam, there is a small core of essential beliefs and practices, so you simply recite what all Muslims believe, and you do what all Muslims do. You could teach it in fifteen minutes. There's no real confusion about what it takes to be a Muslim.

Or a Buddhist. There is a complex view of reality and an eightfold path, but the average Buddhist doesn't attempt to seriously lead "the Buddhist life." That's for monks. My students from Buddhist countries bring an entirely different understanding when they hear a Christian talk about the need to take God seriously. The Buddhist students wonder why serious Christians aren't meditating and chanting all day in a monastery. Why are we working regular jobs? If we were serious about religion, we'd withdraw from the world.

But with Christianity, it's not so easily cut and dried. What do Christians do? Can you imagine all the different answers to that question? On the one hand, it can be quite simple: Repent. Believe. Love.

On the other hand, living the Christian life can be dauntingly complex. If you don't believe me, just check the theology section of a seminary library for all the details. From this standpoint, living a devoted Christian life is best left entirely to monks, nuns, professors, and the supersaints. From the number of books on basic Christianity out there—and the number of people who've read them and still don't get it—there seems to be a good amount of confusion over the basics.

The first time I taught a discipleship course at a church, Charles came to see me after about a month. He wanted to tell me he was quitting the class. That struck me as strange, because Charles was a faithful participant whom everyone in the group admired.

This class emphasized daily time in prayer, scripture memory, accountability, learning evangelistic presentations, identifying spiritual gifts, and discipling other believers. So what was Charles's reason for quitting?

"This is for preachers, not for me," he said. "I've not been called into the ministry."

Christians don't know how to live a Christian life. Some of us aren't even sure we're supposed to. After all the books and studies and sermons, vast numbers of us are still looking for a way to get started.

Why do books such as *The Purpose Driven Life, The Prayer of Jabez,* and *Your Best Life Now* sell millions of copies? They seem to promise a way for ordinary Christians to actually live this life they keep hearing about. Readers are hoping that, finally, they can stop making it up, actually learn their part, and be a Christian. They have the same expectations when they hear a sermon or attend a Christian concert, a retreat, or a church program: this will do it for me.

When it doesn't happen, many of those Christians leave the church. They decide that it's better to admit defeat and have integrity than to pretend to know what they are doing and live as a hypocrite. And I'm right there with them. One hundred and ten percent. In fact, I believe a massive tidal wave of disillusionment is gathering within evangelical Christianity. Millions of people who feel they have been misled will leave the megachurches, abandon organized Christianity, and adopt a personalized, designer approach to faith. Finally, they will leave all the "This is finally, really, truly *it*!" hype far behind.

Evangelical leaders have become so good at propping up the shallow and confused that they have failed to ask what happens when thousands discover they've been scammed. I can tell you what the people in the pew are going to do: leave, and they'll leave with little intention of even looking back, much less going back.

The stage of Western culture is crowded with Christians delivering rehearsed, made-up lines. Almost none of it sounds like Jesus. Virtually none of it acts like Jesus. The average non-Christian long ago made his or her decision that if this act is the closest you can get to the real deal with Jesus, then there is no real deal. Let's move on to something else.

JESUS FANDOM VERSUS DISCIPLESHIP

Bob is a friend I've known for more than ten years. Bob considers himself a Christian, has been part of a dozen churches, and still struggles to live out even the basics of the Christian life. Bob has heard it all, over and over. He attended Christian schools and heard thousands of sermons. He is compassionate and has often been involved in ministry to others.

Yet Bob would be the first to tell you that his Christian journey has been a collection of failures punctuated by bursts of enthusiasm and emotion, usually in response to some church event he attended. Bob has logged a few miles "walking the aisle" at Baptist and Pentecostal churches. He's prayed the prayer and gotten revived many times.

Bob and I have talked about his journey. To better understand Bob and the many like him, it helps to picture a person who wants to be a baseball player. He begins attending games. He goes to Cooperstown to the National Baseball Hall of Fame. He buys team jerseys, visits ballparks, and collects baseball cards. He subscribes to all the games on cable. He memorizes statistics, starts a baseball blog, and plays fantasy-league baseball at work.

There is no question that such a person has a sincere interest in baseball, but he's a fan not a player. To be a player, he would join a team. He would practice year-round, not just during baseball season. He would work out regularly with the team while maintaining his own personal training schedule. He'd learn to throw, catch, hit, and pitch. He would learn the strategy of baseball, how to hit the cutoff man, steal bases, sacrifice to advance a base runner—all the fundamentals of the game. He would master actual game situations. He would study hitting with a hitting coach.

A player can still be a huge fan of the game, but his actual participation in baseball is what allows him to say, "I am a baseball player" and not just, "I love baseball." He might be a poor player, but he'd be a player. Even if he strikes out, he still knows who he is and what he is.

There is a world of difference between any player and any fan. Put a fan on the field in a game, and unless he's lucky, all the fan devotion in the world won't produce a bunt, a pinch-hit single, or a great throw from third to first.

I'd suggest that Bob, like many American Christians, is facing something that wasn't part of the first-century Christian world: mistaking Jesus fandom for Jesus discipleship.

When the New Testament was written, it was dangerous to be a fan of Jesus. It wasn't wise to wear a Christian T-shirt. The latest Christian music wasn't playing on anyone's iPod. Christian gift stores and book nooks couldn't be found. Christian conferences didn't fill ancient stadiums with first-century believers who came to hear celebrity Christian speakers.

In the early years of the church, if you were baptized and confessed Christ, you were frequently checking to see if your head was still attached to your body. You had relatives in prison, and your last pastor was likely a martyr. If you were revealed to be a worshiper of Jesus, it was considered political treason and led to economic ruin—if not worse. You became a target. Because your beliefs violated both the tradition of emperor worship and the laws of Judaism, you were likely to be blamed for any tragedies or natural disasters. And you didn't have the option of taking comfort in reading the words of the New Testament. Even if you were literate, if you saw a scroll of one of the Gospels a few times in your life, you were fortunate.

In the ancient world, the Jesus-shaped life emerged out of the deep transformation of identity that occurred when a person was declared to be a Christian. It was a high-risk life, so being a fan was not an option.

The same thing is happening today in China, India, and the Muslim world. In those societies, there is no Christian subculture that allows a person to participate in a Christian life that amounts to little more than expressing a preference for a particular type of religious entertainment. In those societies, if you aren't willing to suffer, go to prison, or die, you aren't going to be a Christian. If you are a Christian, the realities of your world will compel you toward the life of a disciple.

German Christian martyr Dietrich Bonhoeffer said that "when Christ calls a man, he bids him come and die."[1] Christians might very well read Bonhoeffer's words and say, "I don't get it" or "Well, what he really means is…" Even though it echoes Jesus' call in the Gospels, it's a sentence that doesn't translate well in twenty-first-century American church culture. But read his statement in China or India, and Christians will look at you with clear understanding.

"Of course," they'd say. That outcome is taken for granted.

Blogger Ryan Cordle, writing about the loss of appreciation for the Lord's Supper among evangelical Christians, connected this disconnect to the shallowness of evangelicalism's view of death:

There is a lot of confusion, and perhaps denial and anxiety, about death for the typical Evangelical. This attitude about death takes much of the power of the sacraments away, because the sacraments force us to face death. The story in baptism and the Eucharistic meal is that we all will die, but Jesus has given us the hope of the Resurrection. Yet, if we first refuse to understand our own deaths, then we miss the good news of the sacraments. It's much easier to just "get saved" and then I don't have to think about death any longer, because it is basically all taken care of. However, if we are to grasp the power of the gospel story, then we must somehow grasp that death is part of our own story.

For the early Church, participating in the Eucharist was also a call to (literally) die with Christ. The Eucharist was explaining the reality that to be a Christian is to expect to die for Christ.[2]

My friend Bob and millions of other failed disciples know they are going to die someday if the medicine doesn't work and the health insurance runs out. They also know that to follow Jesus in our culture isn't really serious business, not on the level of risk, life, and death. Instead, it involves having a great life, hearing great music, hanging out at great events, and getting the T-shirt.

A NEW WAY TO BUY FAITH

The Jesus-shaped journey runs directly counter to the primary model of Christianity that dominates the West: consumerism and its false promises. Consumer Christianity invites people to buy Christianity one product at a time. We own it. We wear it. We attend it. We benefit from being around it. Christianity belongs to us. It gives us enjoyment, fun, and status.

What's the menu for a Jesus-follower in a consuming culture?

- Listen to Christian music. Buy it if you like it. Go to the concert.

- Shop for the coolest megachurch. Check out their awesome video technology and kickin' worship band. Enjoy the big screen, the coffee bar, and the free T-shirt. Be amazed at the celebrity communicator they've hired as pastor.
- Go to a conference. Hear the celebrity speakers. Get into the worship music. Twitter the whole event. Wear the T-shirt when you get home.
- Go to a Christian festival. Read a Christian magazine. Check out a Christian movie at the DVD store. What, no T-shirt?
- Listen to Christian radio in your car and on your computer. Download the MP3s. Surf Christian Web sites. Get your information about the world from Christian news programs.
- Buy a new Bible in an edition made just for your niche of the Christian population, like manly men or trendy teens.
- Go to the men's meeting. Go to the small-group meeting. Go to the prayer meeting. Go to the discipleship meeting. Go to the fellowship meeting.
- Take a class in creationism, Christian psychology, Christian dieting, Christian parenting, Christian sexuality, Christian politics, and Christian finances. Buy the materials offered.

If you're not annoyed by now, you're not paying attention. You're annoyed either because you grieve over the commodification of faith or because you think I'm mocking the vast array of proven, people-helping outreach efforts of American evangelicalism. Am I suggesting that all this activity, all this consumption, all these products and events and services don't work together, along with the power of the Holy Spirit, to make us all better Christians?

My answer is simply: Take a look around. What do you think?

Remember my friend Bob? He's done the entire list, three times. He still doesn't know his part in the play. But he did gain a few things. He is weary. He's out a load of cash. He's got a lot of stuff. He's been to a lot of places and heard a lot of things. He has ridden the merry-go-round for years, and he's not getting anywhere.

This morning, if you asked him if he's a Christian, he'd say, "I don't know."

REFUSING TO SELL OUT

We've come to something crucial; something that can't be missed or underestimated in significance. Jesus-shaped spirituality doesn't come in a prepackaged consumer edition. And it doesn't grow out of Christianized consumer culture. The church sign that promises you success if you'll only sign up, join in, attend, participate, and swear the oath is lying. If you're after Jesus-shaped spirituality, you'll discover that it's difficult to find if you keep looking behind the signs and advertisements for the latest product, experience, personality, and worship event.

Jesus-shaped spirituality for Bob, myself, you, and everyone else comes in one form only—in the form of Jesus as we find him presented in Scripture. Jesus hasn't suddenly forgotten how to make disciples, so we can't blame him for the current situation. It's we who are slow to recognize that the life of a disciple doesn't happen at the circus.

We may want to treat discipleship like a product and the process of knowing Jesus like buying a new car. You won't experience Jesus-shaped spirituality with that mind-set.

Like a baseball fan, we may be emotional, devoted, willing to sacrifice, and excited about the game of Christianity. We might even have tender feelings about Jesus. But we won't experience what Jesus said it means to be a disciple if we engage in all the activities of a fan but never become ball players.

It's time to leave behind the life of a fan and commit to becoming a player.

Most of the people who have left the church or are still hanging out in the church, but not understanding why, already know these things. When Jesus talks about what disciples do, how they see the world, and how they live with other people, we realize we've been misdirected. We've been reading the wrong advertisements.

We may be thought of as lost, but we aren't that far away from being exactly where we should be. We simply have to admit the three-ring circus we're living in isn't Jesus' way of making disciples. Consumer Christianity is not what we see in Scripture. Buying a version of the faith is not the approach taken by the Holy Spirit to prod us toward Jesus. None of the Jesus-shaped people in history followed a slick, entertaining, success-driven, celebrity-oriented path to faith and discipleship. A road populated by massive churches, loud music, smooth-talking preachers, media, and meetings is not the road to Jesus-shaped spirituality.

If you need someone to tell you it's okay to feel that way and to be on the outside of all this, then here's my hand. I'm glad to meet you.

Now it's time to take a look at that other road—the narrow, overgrown, largely rejected one—and see where Jesus-shaped spirituality really takes us.

Following Jesus in the Life You Have

There I am, standing in the pulpit wearing a ripped T-shirt and old sweatpants. People are getting up and leaving. I'm trying to preach, but they are clearly upset that I showed up at church with my hair unwashed and my face unshaven and in the clothes of a homeless person.

I preach as fast as I can, but people keep heading for the door. Now it's the choir and the sound crew. At this rate, I'll soon be standing in a dark church, preaching to an empty room.

How did I get here dressed so inappropriately? What was I thinking?

Actually, I didn't. It's one of my recurring stress-related dreams, titled "Inappropriately Dressed, but Still Preaching While People Walk Out." There are versions of this dream in which I'm wearing a bathrobe, gym shorts, and other attire banned from the Sunday wardrobe of a sane preacher.

Stress-related dreams are a regular feature of the lives of many people who struggle with anxieties about their work. I've talked to all kinds of people who know all about dreams where you're late and can't get to your car, or you're supposed to be at an appointment and you can't find a door out of the shopping mall.

One of my recurring dreams has to do with having signed up for a college course—usually biology, for some reason—and suddenly realizing I've forgotten to attend class for several weeks. I have spent money on the tuition, I've been absent, I'm weeks behind, but I have to go back to class and try to catch up. The teacher will be angry, and the students will laugh at me.

How could I forget that I was taking this class? How did I get so distracted? Why didn't I remember something as important as biology?

There's a sick, terrible feeling in the center of this dream, a feeling that is hard to describe. It's like being late, naked, inept, and unprepared— all in one emotional mash-up. I feel like the world's biggest goofball. I can't do anything right.

It's the feeling a lot of people have about discipleship. "I forgot they were even teaching the class. I'm too far behind to start attending now. The teacher will be angry, and the other Christians will laugh at me. I'm worthless. I never can get anything right."

When I wake up from a stress-induced dream, it takes a moment to get reoriented to reality. (Once I dreamed I'd been sent to prison for ten years. It took me a good three minutes to really believe I was not in a cell.)

So wake up, my friend who has left the church or is about to do so. Jesus isn't mad at you. You haven't been tossed into God's Dumpster. You aren't automatically signed up for atheist summer camp because you rejected church-shaped spirituality.

LIVING WHERE JESUS LIVES

I don't know what anyone has told you or said about you…well, I probably do know. But I'm going to tell you that the way of Jesus-shaped discipleship is as open to you as it is to any Christian. In the church, out of the church, heading out of the church, or undecided.

However, let's nail one thing down: my purpose in writing this book is to talk to you as someone who is willing to follow Jesus, not as someone who has decided to give up on Jesus. You may have given up on a kind of religious experience or a particular kind of institutional religion, but you haven't given up on Jesus. I'm not signing anyone's note that says, "Please excuse Johnny. He needs to create his own personal Jesus today." I'm not interested in that option.

We can find Jesus-shaped spirituality if we know where to look and what to look for.

Jesus-shaped spirituality is both personal and communal

Jesus-shaped spirituality grows in the balance between your experience as an individual Jesus-follower and the experiences of a community that you participate in or create. There is no list of ten principles to follow to be a disciple, and I don't have a PowerPoint presentation to sell you. There are no slogans on three-by-five-inch cards to memorize, nor a library of MP3s to listen to. Growing a Jesus-shaped spirituality isn't a matter of learning steps to take or memorizing a diagram. It's much more organic and ordinary than that.

The path to following Jesus hasn't been completely lost in the past two thousand years, despite all the mishandling and demolition. Discipleship is a stubbornly persistent way of life, and we have to begin by seeing where it has always been found. Here are the places to look for Jesus-shaped spirituality:

- It's in your life, with Jesus as Lord. It's the process of knowing God as Jesus reveals him and experiencing the Holy Spirit as Jesus gives him.
- It's a path that follows the Scriptures and leads you to God's ultimate Word of love and meaning for life: Jesus.
- It's growing in your relationships with different kinds of people and in a variety of purposes, but all the relationships give you an opportunity to put Jesus' words and ways into practice.
- It's to be found among experiences that shape you and change you in a Jesus-shaped direction.

- It comes to you as you choose wisdom, discipline, perseverance, and encouragement in following Jesus.
- It's growing a Jesus-centered life in the good soil of repentance, changing your mind to conform to the mind of Christ, and shifting direction from self-centered living to God-anchored living.

All of this is available to you right now, in your life today. Now that we know where to look for it, let's walk the path.

Jesus-shaped spirituality is mentored

This is what Jesus was doing with his disciples: mentoring. It wasn't highly structured, and there was no course syllabus. The disciples learned the Christian life by being with Jesus, and the Jesus-shaped life follows the same route today. It comes to us as we spend time with those who know Jesus and know his way.

You can't live the Jesus-shaped life without mentors. You will find that coming into the many dimensions of knowing Jesus will require many different kinds of mentors: living Christians, authors from long ago, teachers in congregations, servants in different callings, and a great variety of unlikely and overlooked examples of living by faith. Mentors will open up the fullness of Jesus to a person who is ready to be taught and believes Jesus is still teaching and discipling us today.

I'm grateful for what I learned about Jesus from my pastors, but the church-shaped spirituality I inherited from them needed to be balanced with mentors such as Clarence Jordan and Mark Heard, whom I've known only through books and recordings. I've spent hours with mentors like Martin Luther and Charles Spurgeon, whom I could never know without their writings. I've learned from dozens of Bible teachers and many simple servants who embraced what it means to serve the least and the last in the poverty-saturated area where I live. Many of these are names that Jesus knows but the world will never notice.

My mentors include authors such as Timothy George, Robert Capon, and Paul Zahl, who have helped me understand the gospel, and my mother, who showed me what the gospel looks like when it's lived out every day. Gerard Howell mentored me in ministry. Michael McGarvey mentored me in being human. My mentors have been academic teachers, fellow Christians, people who work with their hands, and fathers who showed me how to be a Christian man in a family.

Mentoring can't happen instantly in an eight-week seminar or a weekend conference. It runs at life speed and is played in real time, rewound and replayed with an eye and an ear for the lessons God is teaching. If you aren't willing to be mentored and to put your mentored experience together into an intentional plan to live out the lessons you learn, you won't see the Jesus-shaped life growing in you.

Jesus-shaped spirituality is saturated in the Scriptures

Evangelical Christians are known for carrying large Bibles. It's a bit of a status symbol and a way to say, "We're serious about what God has said."

The phrase *Bible thumper* carries a ton of negative baggage, and deservedly so, considering the damage that has been caused by people who recklessly throw Bible verses around. So I'm aware that aversion to the Bible may be a large part of why some people have left the church. It has been used to beat down dissenters and to justify all kinds of cruelty and oppression that have nothing to do with Jesus.

So we'll acknowledge the baggage, and then we'll set the baggage aside. We can't have Jesus-shaped spirituality without the controlling story of Scripture. That's not about being a Bible thumper, but about learning to think, live, love, and relate to others by using the world of Scripture as the background. The biblical story is the story that comes into complete focus and fulfillment with the arrival of Jesus. Living as a person who loves the world, forgives those who sin against you, serves the poor, and sacrifices for what is right takes on the definition of a Jesus-shaped life only when it comes out of Holy Scripture.

So we read the Bible, and we don't read it magically but intelligently. We read it with an open heart, not like an engineer, but like a child. We don't dissect it, but we enter into it with our imagination. We want to understand all the Scriptures in light of Jesus. We want to "get it" and be moved by it, not just use it to defend our preferences. We want to be intrigued by Scripture, to be questioned by it, and to understand Jesus in the picture frame of the Bible.

For most Christians, the Scripture-saturated and Scripture-shaped life comes in some form of intentional community that includes the reading of Scripture as a regular rhythm of life. It's not my job to tell you what that community looks like, where to find it, or what your level of participation ought to be. I do know that many of the churches and ministries claiming to be deep in Scripture are, in fact, guilty of not seriously reading or engaging with the Bible. I believe that when you find Christians who don't gather for any purpose without reading Scripture and seeking to hear all of it, you've found a helpful community.

One note about this. Even though Christian fundamentalists like to wave the Bible around and claim its authority, they often do nothing more with Scripture than tell you what they had decided in advance that the Bible has to say. They have a gift for finding in Scripture an imprimatur for their most deeply held biases, prejudices, and trigger points. In contrast, among Catholics, Anglicans, and Lutherans, I've heard the Scriptures read most completely and attended to in the most significant ways. Ironically, these are the groups that for years I was warned against by "Bible-believing" Christians.

Don't fall for the fundamentalist and evangelical sales pitch. They have laid claim to the title "Bible-believing Christian," yet they are notorious for reading the Bible selectively, for preaching repeatedly on a few pet passages, and for zeroing in on isolated verses that seem to support their agenda. So don't assume that their cavalier use of the phrase *biblical*

Christian means what it says. Go to the trouble to find Christians who let the Scriptures speak daily, and who respect the voice of Scripture without predetermining every meaning, teaching, and application.

Jesus-shaped spirituality grows in the context of service and the gospel

In the last century, evangelical Christians parted ways with Christians in mainline churches, in part over suspicions about "the social gospel." Evangelicals came off sounding as if helping people was borderline unbiblical. In a classic case of failing to let Jesus set the definition of "normal," many Christians concluded that focusing too heavily on serving the needs of suffering people clouded the gospel message. They felt that Jesus' return was near, and since Christians had a limited time to get everything done, the proclamation of the gospel had to be given sole priority. Somehow, meeting the real needs of disadvantaged people took a backseat or got kicked off the bus completely.

If you read the Bible, you know that Jesus-shaped spirituality lives in both worlds—the spiritual and the physical. Or to look at it a different way, the world is spiritual, even the physical realm. God is everywhere. When Jesus lived on earth, he blessed ordinary places with his presence. It's holy to help people with their very real, ordinary, tangible needs.

Jesus didn't just go about doing good. Jesus proclaimed and enacted what it was like for God's Kingdom to be present on earth. The hungry were fed. The sick were healed. The message and experience of being included and accepted came into real lives. So a Jesus-follower serves others with the Good News of the gospel as well as with justice, peace, and wholeness. Jesus told us: "The Kingdom of heaven is at hand" and "I saw Satan fall like lightning."[1] The Kingdom is here, and the dead are raised, the sick are healed, lepers are cleansed, and prisoners are set free. The Kingdom is here, and sin's hold on the world is reversed. That's the description of Jesus' time on earth, when he spent so much of his life out among people and in their lives.

The Jesus-shaped life isn't the occasional foray into the world followed by months of safety behind the walls of the Christian ghetto. The Christian's life as a disciple is lived in the world. A disciple prays in the world, is useful in the world, and works for God's Kingdom in the world. So find places to serve officially and unofficially. Be the one whose life consistently takes up the servant's role.

When my mother lost her husband and my dad, she moved into a senior-adult high-rise apartment building. For the next thirteen years, my mom served the women who lived on her floor. Even after she lost much of her eyesight, she continued delivering mail, making calls, stopping by to check on neighbors, calling to say hello, listening, and doing favors. She loved being a servant for Jesus on that hallway where sixteen people lived.

My mom attended a megachurch and enjoyed it, but life in the high-rise was her Jesus-shaped path to walk. No church program told her to do this. No church program trained her or listed her as a deacon (or even a deaconess). She never got a plaque, just lots of love and hugs. No one but God knows all she did for her fellow residents.

I am in awe of how Jesus-shaped my mom's life was in her senior years. I was with her when she died, and I thought how she had grown from a gawky farm girl into a beautiful sacrament of Jesus Christ over eighty years, serving him in anonymity and faithfulness, putting most of us who call ourselves "ministers" to shame.

Be like that. Find a community that encourages servant Christianity. Wherever God places you, make it the place you serve him. Whenever possible, seek out the little corners of darkness and pain in our world. Go there and the Jesus-shaped path will rise up to meet you.

While crowds rush to a megachurch to be entertained, you go to the poor, the obscure, and the forgotten. No one will put you on television to say how great you are, but you will discover that when Jesus said, "Truly, I say to you, as you did it to one of the least of these my brothers, you did it to me,"[2] he was pointing the way to the Jesus-shaped life.

I was interviewed on a radio show a few months ago, and the host was prodding me a bit, since I'm known as a critic of the institutional church. He asked me where to find a really good church. He was out of church and didn't want to go back. My answer to him was simple: Go to the poor. Go to the storefront church. Go where they have no money to spend on technology. Go where the hungry are next door and the addicted are on the sidewalk outside. Go there, and you'll find Jesus. You may not find cushioned seats or a free gym, but Jesus will be there.

You knew that, didn't you? The Jesus-shaped way was there, and you didn't need a PhD to find it. The good news is that there are many other pilgrims on the same journey who will see that way as well. Find them. Help one another.

Jesus-shaped spirituality is found in relationships

That sounds trite, doesn't it? Well, stand by. It's big.

Blogger and psychologist Dr. Richard Beck writes at the blog Experimental Theology. In a recent post, he told the story of meeting with a student who said she wanted to "work on her relationship with God." Beck stunned her with his reply: "Why would you want to do that?"

Startled she says, "What do you mean?"

"Well, why would you want to spend any time at all on working on your relationship with God?"

"Isn't that what I'm supposed to do?"

"Let me answer by asking you a question. Can you think of anyone, right now, to whom you need to apologize? Anyone you've wronged?"

She thinks and answers, "Yes."

"Well, why don't you give them a call today and ask for their forgiveness. That might be a better use of your time than working on your relationship with God."

Beck continues: "Obviously, I was being a bit provocative with the student. And I did go on to clarify. But I was trying to push back on a strain of Christianity I see in both my students and the larger Christian culture. Specifically, when the student said, 'I need to work on my relationship with God,' I knew exactly what she meant. It meant praying more, getting up early to study the Bible, to start going back to church. Things along those lines.... Personal acts of piety and devotion are vital to a vibrant spiritual life and continued spiritual formation. But all too often 'working on my relationship with God' has almost nothing to do with trying to become a more decent human being.

"The trouble with contemporary Christianity is that a massive bait and switch is going on. 'Christianity' has essentially become a mechanism for allowing millions of people to replace being a decent human being with something else, an endorsed 'spiritual' substitute."[3]

Jesus-shaped spirituality doesn't replace loving and serving people in relationships with religious piety, political noisemaking, or stroking your ego. The waitress serving you lunch, the nurse at the lab, the co-worker at the next desk, the stranger in the grocery line—these are all people who give you opportunities for Jesus-shaped spirituality to come alive. Consider the following:

- What speaks more loudly of grace: your theological definition of the word *grace* or the tip you leave at dinner?
- What speaks more loudly of your awareness of God: how you sing a praise chorus at church or how you treat your child when he says he is attracted to someone of the same gender?
- What speaks more profoundly of your connection to Jesus: your politics or your willingness to serve kids in the local public school?
- What is Jesus more attuned to: your ability to give a great testimony or your willingness to walk the halls of a nursing home?

You can be sure that the crowd that denounced you for leaving church is highly annoyed at the list I just presented. They believe it's a false dichotomy to think this way, but is it really?

Why do Jesus' parables never refer to rabbis and religious leaders except in instances where those leaders are doing the exact wrong thing? Why did Jesus choose fishermen, not theologians, as the leaders of his movement?

Why is it that women are the constant focus of Jesus' acts of inclusion? Women didn't matter much more than a lawn chair in the first-century world that Jesus inhabited.

Why does Jesus say we have to become like servants, slaves, and children—the classes of people who were "zeroes" in first-century Palestine—if we are to be great in the Kingdom of God?

Why did Jesus wash the feet of his disciples and say that he was leaving them an example to follow? Was he speaking literally or merely figuratively as he passed on a new religious ritual?

Jesus-shaped spirituality doesn't happen in a cute video clip. It happens when families forgive, when fathers hug their wayward children, when couples go to marriage counseling, when you give a waitress a twenty instead of a five, and when grace saturates relationships and then goes looking for more relationships to baptize.

In the next chapter, we have one more area of Jesus-shaped spirituality to explore. We are about to consider the hardest part of the journey. After all I've said about the church, it's time to cross that bridge and ask what place Christian community—the church—has in Jesus-shaped spirituality.

If you are a church-leaver or are about to leave, I promise this isn't a bait and switch. I believe it will be, for many, a most hopeful open door to new ways of thinking about what it means to be a Christian.

Some Help for the Journey

In this final chapter, I'll try to do three things. First, issue a brief warning about what you can expect. Second, include some theologically oriented questions and answers to clarify issues I've raised in the book. And finally, give you some parting words as we set out on our journeys.

The first time I ever asked this question in public—"If I spent three years with Jesus, how would I feel about...whatever?"—I was ridiculed. I've learned that when questions come up regarding contemporary ministry, church growth, success, and the life of faith, Jesus-shaped Christianity doesn't have much value in the minds of many church-shaped Christians. The questions that you and I find so compelling can sound awkward to those who don't believe Jesus belongs at the center of the discussion.

I'd love to tell you that a Jesus-shaped, Jesus-connected Christianity is selling well these days, but I'm afraid that's not the case. And I don't expect the situation to change in the near future.

Why? You have to realize that just as you have left the church to maintain your integrity as a believer, a lot of people have stayed with institutional Christianity for a variety of reasons. Maybe it's where they make their living, or they are tied to tradition, or they are meeting the expectations of their community or the demands of their family. For many of the "stayers," they may be sticking with the church at the cost of their integrity as Jesus-followers.

As with any circumstance where your everyday life is not fully congruent with your faith, people make compromises and rationalizations. In order to maintain a form of Christianity that is acceptable in the church environment, many Christians settle for investing themselves deeply in church-shaped Christianity. It's a type of Christian expression where Jesus makes necessary appearances as a sponsor but rarely, if ever, calls the whole business into question.

I love the book of Revelation's second and third chapters. The resurrected Jesus speaks to seven first-century churches, giving each an individual evaluation and some instructions. Here we are, not even seventy years from the time of Jesus' leaving earth, and there are already a handful of big churches that Jesus can describe in the following terms:

> But I have this complaint against you. You don't love me or each other as you did at first! Look how far you have fallen! Turn back to me and do the works you did at first. If you don't repent, I will come and remove your lampstand from its place among the churches.[1]

> But I have a few complaints against you. You tolerate some among you whose teaching is like that of Balaam, who showed Balak how to trip up the people of Israel. He taught them to sin by eating food offered to idols and by committing sexual sin. In a similar way, you have some Nicolaitans among you who follow the same teaching. Repent of your sin, or I will come to you suddenly and fight against them with the sword of my mouth.[2]

> I know all the things you do, and that you have a reputation for being alive—but you are dead. Wake up! Strengthen what little remains, for even what is left is almost dead. I find that your actions do not meet the requirements of my God. Go back to what you heard and believed at first; hold to it firmly. Repent and turn to me again. If you don't wake up, I will come to you suddenly, as unexpected as a thief.[3]

I know all the things you do, that you are neither hot nor cold. I wish that you were one or the other! But since you are like luke-warm water, neither hot nor cold, I will spit you out of my mouth! You say, "I am rich. I have everything I want. I don't need a thing!" And you don't realize that you are wretched and miser-able and poor and blind and naked.[4]

It's astonishing to hear Jesus speak to first-century Christians this way, and even more astonishing to read his invitations to these churches: to return to Jesus himself. Over and over, the same invitation: return to me.

Less than a century after God came to earth in human flesh, church-shaped spirituality was already deeply affecting the church, turning it into something Jesus refused to endorse. The Jesus Disconnect was so serious that the most quoted part of these chapters is a simple invitation to have a relationship with Jesus by inviting him into the places where he had been excluded. "Look! I stand at the door and knock. If you hear my voice and open the door, I will come in, and we will share a meal together as friends."[5]

The decision to pursue Jesus-shaped spirituality won't take you to a building with a sign out front. You may have to look hard to see the overgrown path of the "road less traveled by...that has made all the difference."[6]

You will be cutting against the grain and swimming against the current. You may find yourself far outside the doors of many churches and thrown in with whomever the scapegoats of the hour happen to be. You should expect to be called liberal, emerging, naive, rebellious, and un-saved. Heads will shake and fingers will wag. But you're in good com-pany. Jesus' own family raised questions about his stability.

If you do not have a greater desire to be loyal to Jesus than to be ac-cepted by the religious establishment, the road may be impossible. Your mentors in following Jesus will often be rebels like yourself. Your new community may not fit the criteria of acceptability imposed by the theological police. Your faith will likely be questioned, and you may experience moments of suffocating doubt and discouragement.

While Jesus-shaped spirituality is the pursuit of humility, the Jesus-follower must have the quiet confidence that following Jesus, both inside and outside the church, is the right road no matter what the critics may say.

My desire for you is that you never give up on following Jesus, whether you are alone or in the company of supportive friends. And even if you feel alone, trust me that you are not alone. There are millions like you, coming from every possible church, experience, school, ministry, and family in Christendom. I believe your presence is changing the landscape of the Western Christian world.

As you pursue a Jesus-connected and Jesus-shaped experience of God, new things are going to happen. As we continue to witness the collapse of much of what remains of standard-issue Christian culture, you will help create a new Christianity. I am excited to see what God does with the people who have read and resonated with this book.

QUESTIONS ABOUT FOLLOWING JESUS

I want to engage some questions and answers on some of the issues this book has raised.

Do you believe that just any gathering of Christians—say two guys talking in a coffee shop—is a church?

Jesus started a movement, and a movement has various levels of organization. Some are more formal and intentional than others. If we don't accept the less-than-churchy forms of the movement as being valid, we miss a massive amount of what Jesus is doing in the world.

There are some instances where there may be only a handful of Christians in a certain setting—a place of employment, a neighborhood, a city, or even an entire country. If they meet to pray for, encourage, and support one another, that's what Jesus had in mind. There are obviously higher levels of organized life in this movement, which we see in the later books of the New Testament. Some Christians are appointed as pastors, deacons, evangelists, and teachers. Of course, in Revelation chapters 2 and 3, Jesus tells some of those large and organized churches that he has nothing to do with them, even though they looked like great churches on the outside.

So I'd be very careful with the idea that only the most self-defined, formally recognized institutions get to make the call on what qualifies as Jesus' movement. I resonate with the Lutheran understanding that church exists where the Word of God is preached and the sacraments are administered. I see all sorts of smaller movements leading up to or participating in that definition. Jesus sees his church in a gathering of two or three followers, and he sometimes doesn't see it in the biggest church in town. So think like Jesus and have some humility on this subject. I encourage each of us to pray: "Lord show me your church as you see it."

Are you antichurch or antidenominations? Do you believe Christians should abandon denominational churches?

It doesn't take a scholar to understand what the New Testament says the church is supposed to be doing. If a church isn't supporting and growing disciples, isn't crossing cultures with the gospel, and isn't encouraging and producing Jesus-followers, I believe you're entitled to look for a different form of community that is doing these things. And it might not be an official-looking church or a group that's affiliated with a recognized denomination.

It's wrong to try to silence or caricature Christians whose churches have failed them. If someone doesn't find Jesus inside an established church and chooses to leave, what is gained by labeling that person as carnal, or spiritually immature, or out of fellowship with God? I trust individual Christians—including those who have left the institutional church or are on the verge of leaving—to know where God wants them to be.

Modern denominations have done a rather amazing thing. They've taken the scandal of rejecting other believers over various doctrines—usually secondary doctrines such as modes of baptism or the question of whether to ordain women—and used it to defend and justify divisions in the church. In other words, they make a lot of noise about minor externals as a way to advertise that Jesus actually endorses their brand of church. They go even further to suggest that God wants you to avoid all the others, since the others (those who baptize babies and use wine in communion) don't have God's full endorsement.

That's a rather brilliant approach to self-justification, but you shouldn't buy it. Denominational labels will tell you very little about whether the people in a congregation are all about Jesus or are blissfully disconnected from him. Any of us who are part of denominational Christianity know that you have to look closer than the ad campaign.

I want every Christian to find a Jesus-shaped community that is doing what the New Testament says a church should do. I don't believe the Christian life happens entirely at church or is determined by what churches decide to do. Christians follow Jesus into the world as disciples on the mission Jesus gave us. The best churches facilitate the mission of Jesus and grow Jesus-followers who pursue that mission.

Your view of the Christian life seems to give people permission to sin freely and to assume that God's grace covers their sins, no matter how serious. Haven't you made it all too easy for people to do whatever they want and to still consider themselves Christians?

This is a longstanding debate in the Christian family. We can't even start to work it out here. I'm mostly a follower of Martin Luther on what the Christian life is like. I have two big interests.

First, I'm interested in honesty. The claims that Christians have lives that work better and turn out better than the other guy are false, as story after story in the Bible illustrates. Judas lived with Jesus for three years, then turned betrayer and hanged himself. Paul had a chronic and painful illness or injury that plagued him every day. Stephen, a tremendous evangelist, was killed by stoning. Mary was widowed before she turned fifty. John the Baptist was beheaded, and his head was then used as a stage prop in a lascivious dance for the entertainment of a pervert. We could enlarge the list, but you get the point. A Christian is never guaranteed earthly honor, material success, health, longevity, or security. Jesus told us that God sends rain to water the fields of both the just and the unjust. He added that if you follow him, you can look forward to hardship.[7]

So Christians need to start being honest, which you'd think would rank at least among the top five priorities for most Christians. But that's not the case. For some reason, Christians can't stop misrepresenting what happens in a Christian's life. It's like believers feel that God should have given his children a leg up on the competition, with better earthly benefits, so they talk like that's what he did. But he didn't.

Let's tell the truth. We are sinful human beings living by faith. Whatever we believe about transformation or holiness, it doesn't take away the fact that Christians are sinful, broken people waiting on the power of the Holy Spirit now and the resurrection later. This is the very realistic and hopeful message of the New Testament: Jesus came to save sinners. That is the Good News. It's time for Christians to stop feeling and acting superior, making it known how great we are, how much we know, and how we have every problem solved. It's gotten to where honest people can't stand to be around us. Jesus-shaped spirituality calls off the pretense regarding what we are really like and creates a community of vulnerable, recovering people.

Second, I'm interested in the gospel, the Good News of Jesus. We aren't in the behavior-modification business. We aren't called to give advice. We aren't entertainers or intellectuals. We have a message about a Jewish peasant, a man who was considered a criminal, died for all sins, and was raised from the dead because he is the Lord of the universe and God in the flesh. In him, God makes the world right and gives us an unconditional, gracious, loving adoption into his eternal family. Whatever transformation happens in someone's life grows out of that message about Jesus. We need to be relentlessly simple and focused. We need to be honest in confessing that we're abject sinners, and that's why we need the gospel.

Gospel honesty. That's what Jesus gives us. The Good News that we aren't good enough to be Christians. The truth is that we are so messed up that we have no other choice but to be Christians.

What do you mean that the only God you know and worship is the One who reveals himself in Jesus? Are you rejecting the Trinity?

The single most audacious Christian claim is that we know God uniquely because he has revealed himself to us through his Son, Jesus. If you get this wrong, the New Testament self-destructs like the audiotapes in the old *Mission: Impossible* television show.

All Christians believe the Trinity is relational and functional; in other words, it's the way God is, and it's the way God works. Jesus' role as the eternal Son of God is to reveal the Father and to do all of the Father's will. He's like an executive officer and official spokesperson all in one.

The reason it sounds provocative for me to say I believe only in the God whom I know as Jesus is because

1. many Christians have little idea that the Trinity is anything more than a theological concept that their pastor tries to explain once a year by using strange terminology (Triune God, three Persons of the Godhead) and illustrations (the egg, the apple, the shamrock);

2. most Christians are sloppy in how they talk about God; and

3. we don't read the Bible carefully enough, especially the gospel of John—in the fourth gospel, you can't go two verses without Jesus saying he came to uniquely reveal the Father.

I could fill up many pages with Scripture references that say "Jesus reveals God as Father." In my own journey, there have been moments when God is inscrutable and hard to understand or even to think about. Thinking about Jesus as the Good Shepherd or as the One who gently restores sinners is very helpful to me at those times. What we believe about God is the most important truth we believe, and it's the one truth that does the most to shape us. God is the Sun too bright for us to see. Jesus is the Prism who makes the colors beautiful and comprehensible.

In the book of Job, Job often calls out to God for an explanation of his suffering. Job repeatedly asks for someone to come and be his advocate with God, to make this terrible experience one of justice and not rejection. Job famously says: "For I know that my Redeemer lives, and at the last he will stand upon the earth."[8]

The Redeemer whom Job sought later stood on the earth as Jesus. He doesn't answer all our questions, but in Jesus we know what God is like, and this is life's greatest gift when we're in the midst of suffering. For the Christian, God isn't an endless mystery but a face and heart we know as identical to Jesus of Nazareth.

I believe in Jesus. He is God to me and for me. I most definitely believe God is Trinity and that the Trinity is an essential core component and basic requirement of Christian orthodoxy. But the gospel calls me to believe in and follow Jesus the Revealer and Mediator who brings God's Kingdom into history. Jesus is God's great Mediator, Messenger, Prophet, Advocate, and Incarnation. The answer to every question about God ends with "Here's what we know because of Jesus."

You call fundamentalists and evangelicals to task for losing track of Jesus. As you do that, are you giving Catholics, Episcopalians, and mainline Protestants a free pass?

Evangelicals are my tribe, but I've had many opportunities, through InternetMonk.com especially, to interact with people from other Christian traditions. My wife is Roman Catholic. I was a supply preacher in the Presbyterian Church (U.S.A.) for more than twelve years. I began my ministry career among Methodists, and I frequently worship with Anglicans.

There are many reasons for evangelicals to take a second look at the mainline churches and the Catholic/Lutheran/Anglican tradition. These denominations have made their own mistakes and errors, but they have conserved many things evangelicals can benefit from. For example, most Baptists can't identify or recite the Apostles' Creed. Aside from Christmas and Easter, the Christian year is almost unknown in evangelicalism. Public readings of Scripture are seldom part of evangelical worship, while "liberal" mainline churches will read two or three Scripture lessons in worship every Sunday. These and many other elements of the larger, older, deeper Christian tradition are still at work in many nonevangelical churches.

Of course, many of these churches have engaged in serious biblical compromise on issues that most evangelicals believe are essentials, especially issues of gender and sexuality. So I am in no way giving a blanket approval to the mainline churches.

I see the Christian world like this: we've inherited a divided map of the truth, and each of us has a piece. Our traditions teach us that no one else has a valid map and that our own church's piece shows us all the terrain and roads that exist. In fact, there is much more terrain, more roads, and more truth for us to see if we can accept and read one another's maps, fitting them together to give us a clearer picture of the larger Christian tradition.

I come from an evangelical background, but I understand that the movement Jesus began exists in many different places, including where I've been told—sincerely but wrongly—that Christ cannot be found. One expression of my confidence in Christ is my awareness of his presence among other Christians, even those with whom I have serious disagreements. That's been my journey, and I'm very grateful that it has allowed me to value my own tradition while seeing the value in others.

I would assume that since you are distancing yourself from institutional evangelical Christianity, that you no longer accept the evangelical label for yourself. What do you suggest we call the brand of Christianity you're advocating?

There are several impulses in Protestant Christianity that create labels. There is the Reformation itself. There are the historical, cultural, and theological roots of various groups. There is the desire to return to the Christianity of the first century and the quest to more fully participate in the reality of the present.

From all of this come denominational names, theological labels, and various descriptions of teams, tribes, and movements. The overall effect is disorienting, and Roman Catholic and Eastern Orthodox believers are understandably embarrassed.

At the same time, labels help us separate out some things that matter. They assist us in shedding the nonessential and focusing in on a proper goal. So while I have no desire to sell a label for a movement, there are some descriptors that I find helpful. Whether they are helpful to anyone else is a matter of personal preference.

Jesus-shaped spirituality is a spirituality that I am convinced Jesus himself would recognize. Its source is Jesus as presented in the gospel, and its measurement is asking Jesus-related questions before you ask any others.

The term *post-evangelicalism* describes a movement of those who desire to move past what they see as the failure of contemporary evangelicalism and to draw on the resources of larger, deeper, more ancient Christian tradition as material for evangelicalism's future.

I call myself a reformation Christian to purposely not identify with a denomination but to say that the Reformation was a tragic necessity and its impulses toward Scripture rather than church tradition are sound and to be valued.

Often I describe myself as a post-evangelical, reformation-loving Christian in search of a Jesus-shaped spirituality. That wouldn't fit easily on a T-shirt, so it probably won't catch on. And anyway, I don't wear message T-shirts.

A BLESSING FOR YOUR JOURNEY

Finally, a word as we go our separate and similar ways. It would be presumptuous of me to assume that I know everything about following Jesus. There is nothing helpful about a confidence that is born of a desperate desire to be right or to be heard. Our confidence is always humbly placed in Christ himself.

The disciples sometimes got it very right, and Jesus rejoiced with them. "I saw Satan fall like lightning."[9] They also sometimes got it very wrong, and Jesus said, "How long must I be with you?"[10]

If someone writes a book to say "Follow these ten ideas, and you'll get it right in following Jesus," I'd say they have a lot to learn about themselves and what it means to be a disciple. It's a long road, and no one person's map—or reading of Scripture—tells you everything you will encounter along the way. For this reason, I've discovered that many of the most consistently Jesus-shaped people are not telling anyone what to do. They are not selling tickets or giving lectures. They are, instead, living the life, a life that won't be seen if you look only at the official press releases of churchianity.

The Jesus-shaped life is found where Jesus would be found. Sitting in a coffee shop talking to a single mom who waitresses to make a living. Going to India to learn about ministering to the poorest of the poor. Faithfully working in an inner-city food bank that serves thousands who lost their jobs. Leading a worship service for the elderly at a nursing home.

Taking in medically challenged foster kids. Counseling the unemployed at a church-based community center. Running an Upward Soccer league in a housing project. Putting feet on a neighborhood prayer ministry that goes door to door to pray with anyone who asks. Starting a storefront church in a neighborhood that traditional churches have abandoned. Volunteering to teach immigrants how to fill out job applications. Serving as the volunteer coordinator of the county hospice.

The Jesus-shaped life is found in a forgotten mission where only ten elderly women show up on Sundays. In a nursing-home chapel and a prison Bible study. The Jesus-shaped life is starting a church in the inner city, rather than the suburbs, and reaching out to street people and the poor, not the white, upwardly mobile middle class.

In the church. Out of the church. Working with the church. Working where the church doesn't like to go. Stretching the influence of the gospel outside the comfort zone of the usual. Being a witness to the church of what Jesus would be doing.

The practitioners of Jesus-shaped spirituality are not all reading from the same book or wearing the same uniform. They are not clones of one another or products of some merchandized movement. They are Jesus-followers and Spirit-listeners, drawn into the world as they are drawn to follow after Christ.

The path of Jesus-shaped spirituality has taken them into, out of, and sometimes back into the church, but always more and more in imitation of Jesus, both in his compassionate actions and in the movement and community he creates. It starts churches in unlikely places and stays with churches that are dying. It walks away only when following Jesus requires them to make such a choice.

As I have come to discover that Jesus' Kingdom is a far more diverse and interesting movement than I realized when I was growing up in narrow fundamentalism, I've come to understand that what Jesus is doing in the world is exactly what his parables described: the smallest of seeds growing into a great tree.[11]

Many of us will meet one another on this journey. We may share the same story or the same pain, or we may be so different that we keep looking, again and again, to recognize the family resemblance. It is my hope that the time we have spent together will encourage you to keep pursuing Jesus, no matter where you are in your journey. Don't neglect the search for authentic, Jesus-shaped spirituality.

And finally, when we come home, we will find that Jesus has made us like himself, and yet, amazingly, we will have remained in every way ourselves.

Epilogue

After Michael Spencer's death, his son-in-law found the following journal entry in one of Michael's notebooks. Michael's family thought it would make a fitting epilogue to Mere Churchianity. *They were right.*

December 4, 2009
At approximately 1 p.m. EST, the doctor's office called to tell me there were matters of concern on the CT scan. So no matter how long one has resisted the reality that the journey will take this turn, the turn arrives without permission and without the agreement that I will be able to find some mental tactic to live in denial. The next chapter arrives at its own time with its own contents, and I must open it now.

Like it or not, *this* is what I must live with, worship with, pray with, and love with today. This is my life as it comes to me from God. This is the God I know in Jesus. This is the God who gives my life significance. Whatever I am…or whatever I hope to be comes in the love of this God for me. The day is about receiving God's love; enjoying God's love; placing my many, many fears in God's love. This is today: a new turn, a new chapter, the same loving Father [whom] Jesus called *Abba.*

Every word of the gospel is written to men who will be dead but are now alive by the mercy of God. This is my life and the life of all other persons.

(Michael died April 5, 2010.)

Chapter 1

1. Matthew 28:20.
2. See Revelation 3:20.
3. See Ephesians 5:28–32.
4. Trends and statistics taken from the "U.S. Religious Landscape Survey," published by the Pew Forum on Religion & Public Life. Found at http://religions.pewforum.org/pdf/report-religious-land-scape-study-key-findings.pdf (accessed February 2, 2010).

Chapter 2

1. See Michael Spencer, "The Coming Evangelical Collapse," *Christian Science Monitor*, March 10, 2009. Found at www.csmonitor.com/2009/0310/p09s01-coop.html/ (accessed February 1, 2010).
2. Mark 10:35.

Chapter 3

1. If there are some theologically sensitive souls out there, fear not. I'm a card-carrying member of classic Trinitarian Christianity: Father, Son, and Holy Spirit. One God, always existing as three Persons. Anything less than the Trinity isn't God, because the Bible and the church through the ages are in perfect agreement on that one. But in this chapter we want to recalibrate the compass, and the true north for our journey of Jesus-shaped spirituality is…Jesus.
2. Quotations taken from John 8:58; 5:39, NLT; 6:53; 8:46; 10:30; 11:25; paraphrases of 17:1–8.
3. John 6:68, author's paraphrase.

4. John 14:9.

5. Author's paraphrase of Matthew 28:18–20 and other New Testament quotations of Jesus.

6. Mark 4:41, NLT.

7. 1 Corinthians 8:4–6.

8. 2 Corinthians 10:3–5.

9. See Revelation 3:14–22; 2:8–11.

10. See Matthew 23.

11. Mark 8:34–37.

Chapter 4

1. See 1 Peter 2:11, NLT, 1996 version.

2. See Matthew 6:9–13.

3. Jackson Browne, "The Rebel Jesus," published by BMG Music, 1991. For the complete lyrics to this song, go to www .jrpgraphics.com/jb/tnvyh.html (accessed February 2, 2010).

Chapter 5

1. See Genesis 1:25–28.

2. See Ecclesiastes 3:11.

3. I'm aware that Catholic and Orthodox Christians have a very up-front claim to "connecting" to Jesus via the sacraments, dispensed by the church as the authorized representative of Jesus on earth. I'm writing primarily in an evangelical Protestant context, where claims that the church "connects" us to Jesus are heard in terms of the gospel and the continuing work of the Holy Spirit both in and outside the church.

4. Examples of this abound. It is instructive to reread Jesus' hard words about the cost of discipleship, especially his parables and his response to the man who wanted to care for his father in his old age. (See Matthew 5:43–48; 10:34–39; 22:1–14; Luke 9:59–62.)

Chapter 6

1. See Genesis 1:26–27; Romans 1:19–20; Ecclesiastes 3:11.

Chapter 7

1. See the full story in John 4.
2. "The Nicene Creed," *The Book of Common Prayer,* 1789 (New York: The Church Hymnal Corporation, 1979), 358.
3. Colossians 1:15; 2:9, NLT; John 1:1–18; 3:16.
4. See Genesis 1:25–28.

Chapter 8

1. Mark 1:14–15.
2. Matthew 28:19–20.

Chapter 10

1. For more on this idea, see Alister McGrath, *Christianity's Dangerous Idea* (San Francisco, CA: HarperOne, 2007).
2. See Mark 7:18–20.
3. See John 10:16.

Chapter 11

1. Quote taken from "Rabbit Seasoning," Warner Brothers cartoons, story by Michael Maltese. Distributed by Warner Brothers Pictures, 1952.
2. See 1 Timothy 2:5.
3. Martin Luther, *Luther's Works, Vol. 48* (St. Louis, MO: Concordia, 1965), 281.
4. Mark 10:35.
5. Mark 10:44.
6. See Mark 10:41.
7. See 1 Timothy 2:5.
8. Galatians 2:20–21.

Chapter 12

1. This statement from President Bill Clinton can be heard at www.youtube.com/watch?v=j4XT-l-_3y0 (accessed February 3, 2010).
2. This statement from President Bill Clinton can be heard at www.youtube.com/watch?v=KiIp_KDQmXs (accessed February 3, 2010).
3. 2 Corinthians 4:7–11.
4. 2 Corinthians 12:9–10.
5. Richard Selzer, *Mortal Lessons* (New York: Simon & Schuster, 1976), 45–46.
6. Hermann Sasse, *Jahrbuch des Martin-Luther-Bundes* (Neuendettelsau, Germany: Freimund-Verlag, 1946), 38–42.

Chapter 13

1. See Luke 5:33–39.
2. See Genesis 12:1.
3. See Exodus 3:1.
4. See Genesis 45:1–15.
5. See Matthew 19:21; 8:18–22; Luke 9:57–62.
6. John 3:30.

Chapter 14

1. William Shakespeare, *King Lear,* act 5, scene 3.

Chapter 15

1. The law of averages leads me to assume that many other people in Andrea's church congregation share the same struggles she experiences. So why did it appear to her that she was the only person who was struggling? I have to conclude that most Christians keep their struggles a secret, which leaves everyone else feeling alone.
2. See Mark 7:24–30.

3. See Mark 5:18–20.
4. See John 21:15–19.
5. See Galatians 5:13.

Chapter 16

1. Dietrich Bonhoeffer, *The Cost of Discipleship* (New York: Simon and Schuster, 1995), 89.
2. Ryan Cordle, excerpt from "Death: Why Evangelicals Are Missing the Sacraments," 2 Ages Verging Blog, posted August 8, 2009, http://2ages.blogspot.com/2009/08/death-why-evangelicals-are-missing.html (accessed August 8, 2009).

Chapter 17

1. Matthew 10:7; Luke 10:18.
2. Matthew 25:40.
3. Found at http://www.experimentaltheology.blogspot.com/2009/08/bait-and-switch-of-contemporary.html (accessed August 8, 2009).

Chapter 18

1. Revelation 2:4–5, NLT.
2. Revelation 2:14–16, NLT.
3. Revelation 3:1–3, NLT.
4. Revelation 3:15–17, NLT.
5. Revelation 3:20, NLT.
6. Quoted from Robert Frost, "The Road Not Taken." Found at www.poets.org/viewmedia.php/prmMID/15717 (accessed September 1, 2009).
7. See Matthew 5:45; 10:34–38.
8. Job 19:25.
9. Luke 10:18.
10. Mark 9:19, NLT.
11. See Matthew 13:31–32.